HOW TO CREATE THE STAR OF YOUR FAMILY CULTURE

THE HEAVEN ON EARTH WORKBOOK

# How to Create the Star of Your Family Culture

## The Heaven on Earth Workbook

### With Excerpts from *Heaven on Earth: A Handbook for Parents of Young Children*

## Sharifa Oppenheimer

### Photography by Robert Radifera

SteinerBooks | 2015

Published by SteinerBooks
an imprint of Anthroposophic Press, Inc.
610 Main Street
Great Barrington, MA 01230
www.steinerbooks.org

Photography by Robert Radifera (radifera.com)
book design: William Jens Jensen

PUBLISHED WITH GENEROUS SUPPORT FROM
THE WALDORF CURRICULUM FUND

ISBN: 978-1-62148-139-3 (paperback)
ISBN: 978-1-62148-140-9 (eBook)

# CONTENTS

# INTRODUCTION:
## THE STAR OF YOUR FAMILY CULTURE

I am so glad you are curious and eager to explore creating your own family culture! I would like to share with you some beginning thoughts about how to define Family Culture; perhaps this will be a springboard for you to further consider as you shape your own ideal definition!

In all the activities we do with our children we are making decisions that establish our family's culture. Culture is nothing more or less than the way we live our lives. Although this "culture making" is going on all the time, the quality of the culture pivots entirely on the awareness we bring to it. We are fashioning our family's culture with each decision, so let us bring as much consciousness to this process as we can.

To raise children who, as young adults, can freely create their life as they envision it—this is our task. We do this by fashioning a space in which, with a delicate balance of guidance and freedom, our children can discover who they really are.

With each decision we make, we are showing our children what we value. As adults, we have the capacity to look at each other's choices and know whether we agree with these values or not. Our children have not yet gained this power of discrimination. Because our very young children experience themselves as being at one with their environment, they deeply internalize the value system we offer them. In consciously choosing to value life in all its forms; in choosing to foster health, wellbeing, self-respect, and respect for others, we show our children that we value them. Perhaps more than anything, our young children are alive, like the first day of creation. In showing our children that we value Life, we affirm through every action that we love them, in all their liveliness.

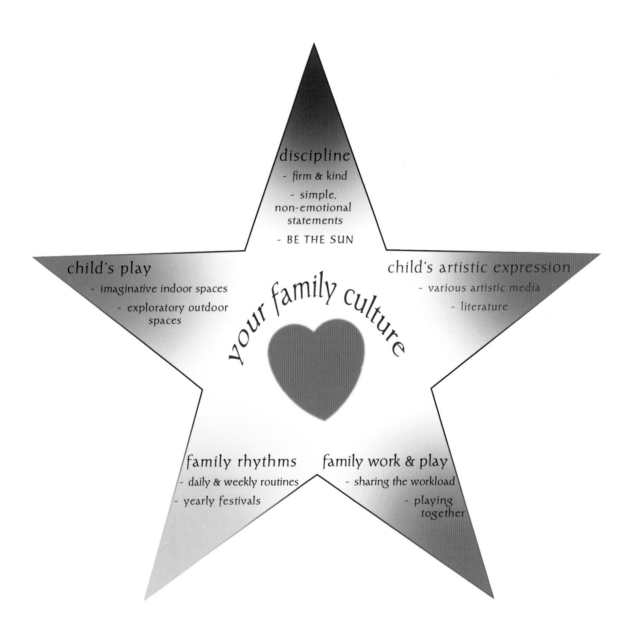

discipline
- firm & kind
- simple, non-emotional statements
- BE THE SUN

child's play
- imaginative indoor spaces
- exploratory outdoor spaces

child's artistic expression
- various artistic media
- literature

your family culture

family rhythms
- daily & weekly routines
- yearly festivals

family work & play
- sharing the workload
- playing together

It is through all the choices we make, large and small, and through actions more than words, that family culture is established. Our children come to learn that they are an essential part of a living organism called "our family." Through this clear sense of family, our children eventually learn the cardinal place they have in the larger family of the world. They know that they belong. At this time, when humanity suffers from the life-negating forces of alienation and disenfranchisement, a sense of belonging is more crucial than it has ever been. (from *Heaven on Earth*)

## *Our Workbook Format*

In this workbook we will explore in depth many of the elements that combine to form family culture. Those of you who have read *Heaven on Earth* are familiar with thinking about these elements as a five-pointed star whose points are:

- Family Rhythms
- Family Work and Play
- Child's Play
- the Child's Artistic Expression
- and Discipline, beginning with the parents' self-discipline.

*In the center of the star, we see the heart of the family, the Love Connection, which is the magnetic pole that holds all these elements in orbit.*

The first two points, Family Rhythm and Family Work and Play, act as the "legs" of the star. They are the foundation; with their strong thighs, they give support and take our family on this journey together. The next two points, Child's Play and the Child's Artistic Expression, are the "arms" of the star. They are sensitive, fine, and nimble. They are the limbs whereby children reach toward the world to discover themselves.

Each of these four major areas, the legs and arms of our family, creates an embodied space for the "head," the self-reflecting aspect, which we can call Discipline. I believe that when these first four

• Think of Family Culture as a subtle membrane, a living veil, that can hold, support, nourish and unite all members of your family into a coherent organic system. This possibility is dependent upon the awareness—*the mind, heart and body awareness*—of the parents. An integrated and coherent family springs from parents who strive for integration and coherence.

• There is no room for perfectionism here! Remember perfection is the enemy of the good. We simply live with joyful striving, and learn to laugh and forgive ourselves. In these pages, we can learn to love our humanness, with all its beauty and forgetfulness.

areas are balanced and functioning well, discipline is established in the subtle atmosphere of the home. This rhythmic, disciplined home, created by the parents' own self-discipline, develops eventually, into a self-disciplined child.

At the heart of the word "discipline," and at the heart of the work we will do together, is the concept of discipleship, which implies "following with love." Our children *do* follow us with love, through their innate capacity of imitation. Whatever state our own heart is in, and whatever the family culture we establish, they will, in their own way, mirror it back to us in their behavior.

• The Love Connection, both between the parents together and between parents and children, is the magnetic pole that holds all the elements of Family Culture in orbit.

• The words discipline and discipleship contain the same root, which implies "following with love" Humans are designed to follow with love, through the miracle of imitation.

• We will work with eight aspects of family life, in eight sections:
  ◦ The Love Connection
  ◦ Family Rhythms
  ◦ Family Work
  ◦ Family Play
  ◦ Child's Artisitic Expression
  ◦ The Wonder of Story
  ◦ Child's Play
  ◦ Discipline through self-discipline

1. In the *first* section we will explore the heart of our Star and the heart of Family Culture, the love connection. Here we will learn the many ways love is foundational not only to the health of our family, but also to the entire developmental scope of childhood. In addition, we will learn a simple tool to help us remain balanced and loving in the midst of our daily rounds.

2. In the *second* section we will study Family Rhythms, which encompasses our various daily and weekly rituals and routines, the celebration of yearly festivals, as well as the hidden power of our own inner rhythms.

3. In the *third* section we will look carefully at Family Work—how we attend to the workload of caring for a family and how we can engender joy in the work.

4. In the *fourth* section we will balance this by discovering the way our family relaxes and plays together. We will also look into the future, to envision how we would like to play together fifteen years from now!

5. In our *fifth* section, we'll explore the Child's Artistic Expression as we not only discuss, but engage in artistic experience.

6. In the *sixth* section, we will learn how to use Story to educate, delight, and nourish our children. And we will learn to create our own "homemade" stories as well.

7. In the *seventh* section, we will explore Child's Play and include the awareness of the crucial place Play holds in the life of every

child. We will also look at the creation of imaginative indoor play spaces and a variety of exploratory outdoor play spaces.

8. Finally, in the *eighth* section we will discuss the role of discipline through the lens of self-discipline. Our children need us to be worthy of their imitation! We will also remember some self-regulation/ self-discipline techniques.

We will explore family culture in eight "sections." You can begin with section one and methodically discover your way through all eight. Alternatively, if your nature is more mercurial, you can glance through the book and decide which topic appeals most, beginning where your interest leads you. Remember that the "legs" of the star are the foundation, and the arms are the creative, exploratory aspect. The head and heart of the star focus on your own inner work.

Each section will include a variety of ways for you to approach the subject:

1. Introductory thoughts, to get you thinking about and considering the subject. Much of this is excerpted from *Heaven*, so will sound familiar to you.
2. Intention. This gives us a way to focus on what we hope to accomplish.
3. Four different ways, one per week if you like, to work interactively with the material, to make it your very own.
4. Weekly *visioning and assessment pages* where you can plan and take notes. This can include *journaling*, as a potent way to make the work personal. So use your pages to your best benefit!
5. Weekly conversation notes: *I think it will be most fun and helpful if you take this journey with your partner, or a group of parents. Isn't part of the fun of any journey to share the vistas, the campfires, and stubbed toes with loved-ones?* In these pages, you can jot down notes from conversations, as reminders and tips.

So, parents—grab your partners and *Let's Get Started!*

---

**Five Ways We Will Explore Each Section Topic**

1. Introductory Thoughts
2. Intention
3. Interactive Exercises
4. Weekly Pages for visioning and assessment
5. Weekly Conversations with Partners

# THE HEART OF FAMILY CULTURE
# THE LOVE CONNECTION

The love connection between parent and child begins in utero; the tones of the mother's voice set the embryo dancing. And the mother's emotional state directly determines the development of the baby's brain. The love connection between the primary caregiver and the child continues to contain and shape the child throughout childhood, but its most profound effects are in the first three years. Mary Aisnworth and thirty years of research in attachment studies show that the mothering style (primary caregiving style) predicts emotional traits in later life. Who we are and how we relate to our child shapes them in long-lasting and measureable ways.

## *Sensitivity and Balance Carry the Day*

Hearing a statement this profound can strike terror in our souls! It would be easy to misinterpret, and feel we now must always be leaned toward our child, never taking our attention away from him. However, attachment theory tells us the parent needs to be sensitively aware and responsive to the child's needs, not overly protective. Like dancing or riding a bike, the needs of the moment will change as the tempo and terrain of life changes for your child. It is our sensitive response to his ever-changing journey that creates the shape of our unique love connection.

As parents, we are the pivot. How we respond on an hourly basis, in the rush of daily life, *who we are*, matters more than anything else to our children. Where do we find the internal balance to accomplish this huge task? How do we develop the necessary

• The Love Connection begins in utero: the embryo dances in response to the tones of the mother's voice. It is an underwater ballet! The way we parent our children, especially in the first three years, predicts their emotional traits later in life.

• No, you don't need to have eyes always and only upon your child, being the "helicopter parent." This can be as damaging, in the end, as neglect. Balance is the key! Sensitive, responsive awareness to the ever-changing growth and needs of our child creates the shape of our unique love connection.

• Who we are and how we respond matters more than we can imagine. Knowing this, where do we find the internal compass to navigate a middle course between "helicoptering" and "free-ranging"? There is only one place: *inside!*

sensitivity to our ever-changing child? Where do the inner resources come from, and how do we keep going, through all the long years of a childhood?

I believe this balance and sensitivity, these resources, are found only internally. I am sure there are other ways to access these inner treasures, but let me tell you how I managed to balance teaching full time, parenting three enthusiastic boys, keeping a home in order and harmony and even having fun!

## The Meditating Brain

The latest and finest part of our brain structure is the pre-frontal cortex, or "angel lobes," the seat of empathy and the ability to care. To respond sensitively to our child's needs, empathy must be cultivated. Empathy is defined as the vicarious experiencing of the feelings, thoughts, or attitudes of another. Isn't this what we need, when our child is in distress: she needs something and is either too young or too upset to find words? We need to *experience* this particular feeling of upset vicariously, to *feel* from the inside what she needs, as well as *know* from the inside which tools will help calm and soothe. Our child needs to "feel felt."[1] When we experience their feeling inside our self, we can begin to know what the remedy is. To know the remedy, though, we have to be in touch with our own feelings and know how to integrate these within our own being.

For me, the path of meditation offers an inner field in which to practice the skills of self-awareness, self-regulation, and integration. Finding my way along this path, I have discovered a wellspring of insight, courage, and strength. Sometimes, in difficult situations, I would open my mouth to say something to one of my sons and be surprised to hear my voice speak wisdom I didn't even know I knew! How can this be so?

There is more and more current research confirming that meditation improves our physical and emotional health, while regular long-term practice actually changes the structures of the brain that control our moods. Contemplative practice strengthens a neurologi-

• Meditation gives us a way to practice self-awareness, self-regulation and integration. A few of meditation's treasures are

◦ Improved physical and emotional health

◦ Mood control

◦ Improved social awareness

◦ Greater compassion for others

◦ The ability to find new perspectives

• Through meditation, we can find the calm center in the midst of the cyclic movements of life.

• Let's be our "best selves" for our children. And remember, no perfectionism here: "best" means self-observing, self-regulating, and self-compassion!

cal circuit that generates social awareness and compassion for others. [2] Mindfulness meditation encourages perspective taking. [3]

Emotional health, mood-control, social awareness, compassion for others and the ability to find a new perspective: we wish there was a pill we could take to offer all these qualities! Really, there is—meditation. However, it requires at least 10 minutes of attention each day. There are many avenues for meditation instruction, and I encourage you to explore possibilities that appeal to you. I will also offer you a simple step-by-step process that I call "Heartfulness" meditation. With a little experience, this can be practiced at any time during the day, and with your eyes open. As parents, especially, and teachers as well, we need a meditation that we can do while fully engaged with the children and with our eyes open! We can find the calm center in the midst of the cyclic movements of life.

If we choose the path of meditation, we have a very real possibility to be our best selves for our children. *Best* does not mean perfect, though. For me, best means self-observation, self-moderation, and *compassion* for my own shortcomings. If I can develop patience for myself, the humility to recognize my mistakes, and resilience to learn from them, then I have a better chance at modeling these qualities as I am in relationship with my children. Heartfulness meditation begins with self-awareness and compassion. This creates a strong, flexible foundation for sensitive awareness and responsiveness with our child.[4]

## Heartfulness Meditation

This is a meditation I have been practicing for nearly forty years. Much to my surprise, I discovered about fifteen years ago, that the Heart Math Institute, www.HeartMath.org, not only teaches a very similar meditation, but also has done hundreds of research studies that validate the physical, emotional, social, and cognitive benefits of a simple heart-based meditation. I have been teaching this warm meditation to groups of parents and teachers for a number of years. I have had the pleasure to receive feedback that affirms how life

**Hearfulness Meditation Instructions**

• Allow your consciousness to rest in your heart.
• Feel the movement of your breath, as your lungs expand and contract.
• Be aware that you are being "rocked" by your breath; this is goodness
• Focus on the feeling of goodness or love, not the concept.
• Stay with this felt-experience of goodness or love.
• As sensation, feeling or thought arises, bring it into the peaceful resonance of this heart-space.
• There is room for all of life in this heart-expanding meditation.

**One further step**

• While in the meditative state, with the eye of your heart, imagine a difficult situation in your family life.
• Bring this difficulty into the peaceful resonance of your heart
• Ask the wisdom of your heart how it can help.

*Your own heart knows the way. Trust it!*

changing and "down-to-earth helpful" this user-friendly practice is. Most significant to this technique, is that *to feel a positive feeling is more important than trying to empty the mind of thoughts.*

It is easiest to begin when you have a bit of quiet time, to get the felt-experience of its simplicity. With just a little practice you can do this with your eyes open, while the children play close by, while you are cooking, while you stand in line at the grocery store, and even when your child is out-of-balance and needy. It is designed to be practiced in the midst of a busy life.

## Heartfulness Instructions

1. In the Western world, we usually experience our consciousness as located in our heads. Allow your consciousness to slowly drift down and settle, resting, in your heart. This is not necessarily the physical heart, but rather the heart center, or the area in the center of your chest. You can rest your hand on this central area if it helps you to *feel* your awareness relaxing in your heart.

2. As you simply notice this heart area, you will become aware of your breath moving through your lungs. This movement of the breath very subtly "rocks" you. Feel your body slightly sway, as if you are in a hammock and being rocked by the breeze.

3. Allow yourself to experience this movement as peaceful and positive. I call this feeling "goodness." Other positive emotions may also arise, including appreciation, harmony, wellbeing, gratitude, and sometimes love. If these emotions do not arise naturally, you can remember when you felt this goodness in a person or occasion. Focus on the *feeling*, not the memory.

4. Now you can remain with the felt-experience of goodness as the breath moves through your heart. Perhaps, like me, you will feel this micro-movement through your whole body and feel the waves of goodness this brings. Notice that this goodness is reflected in a nearly imperceptible smile, perhaps as if your body/soul is smiling.

5.  As thoughts, emotions, and sensation arise, you can bring these experiences into the peaceful resonance of this heart space. Don't follow their "story line," but just allow them to be gently rocked in your heart. There is room for all of life in this heart-expanding meditation. If emotions other than goodness arise, such as sorrow, anxiety, or anger, you can also bring these into your heart space. Within the coherence of the heart, you can allow the breath to move through these negative emotions, as well. Observe and see what effect your rhythmic breath and open heart bring.

6.  When you feel comfortable with this practice, add another step. With your eyes closed, bring a difficult situation into this field of coherence and goodness, perhaps one with your child or within your family. Allow the breath to move through and gently "rock" the difficulty. Now ask your heart what wisdom it can offer to help you in the midst of this situation. Your own heart knows the way. Trust it!

## The Heart is Not Just a Pump!

Here is a little more inspiration to encourage you to attend to the heart of your family culture—your own inner landscape.

In the scientific field of neurocardiology, studies show that our heart is comprised of sixty to sixty-five percent brain cells! When we talk about the "intelligence of the heart" it is not a metaphor; the heart has direct neural connections to the limbic, or emotional, part of our brain, and an ongoing dialog takes place between the two.

When we regulate and "steady" the heart's electromagnetic field through meditative practice, by walking in nature, in prayer, song, or music, the heart's powerful "field of resonance" brings all our physiological systems into harmony and balance. All systems become entrained to the coherence of the heart. Our own state of coherence then brings others we encounter into resonance as well. This is crucial inspiration for parents; the more finely tuned we

> • The Heart is more than a pump: our heart contains sixty to sixty-five percent brain cells. The intelligence of the heart is for real!
>
> • Steadying the heart through contemplative practices brings our whole physiology, which includes sensations, emotions and thoughts, into coherence. Through resonance, our harmonious state of being brings those we encounter into this balanced state, too. When we are simply present and feeling the goodness of the heart, we can bring this gift to our children, our family and all those we meet!

become, the more *coherent* we are. It is simply our presence that brings salutogenesis, a sense of wellbeing, to our family!

*Section One Intention*: to bring awareness to parents of the pivotal place we play in the life of our family. Intention to offer tools of self-knowledge, self- compassion, and self-regulation.

## Week One Interactive Exploration

*This week, we'll begin to experience the meditation and make an image, a personal "map" to guide us back to heartfulness.*

- Choose a quiet time and place to practice the Hearfulness meditation. Quietly breathe through the heart with the felt-experience of goodness. Do this for five to ten minutes.
- On a large piece of crayoning paper, color with crayons the inner experience, the energy, the image of this meditative experience.
- Now sit back and gaze with open awareness at your image. This image is an icon, it is a visual map that brings you back to the felt-experience that heart-coherence brings.
- Take a pen and blank piece of paper. Referring to your icon, write a few lines, a few poetic words, which will act as an affirmation. Put these words and your icon on the refrigerator or bathroom mirror. Perhaps tape them to your computer…give them a place to live in your daily life.
- Throughout the week, take a moment each day to look at the image and your poem; allow them to become a map that takes you to the place where your breath moves through your heart. Gaze and breathe. Let them visually transport you to the goodness heart breathing brings.

---

**Section One Intention**

to learn tools of

- self-knowledge
- self-compassion
- self-regulation

**Week One Exploration**

- Practice the Heartfulness meditation.
- Make a picture, an icon, of your inner experience.
- Write a few poetic lines.
- Post your picture and your poem so they are available to refer to through the week.

*Don't forget to write in your Weekly Pages, and talk with your partners!*

*Weekly Pages*

**Vision and Assessment**: Throughout the week, take a few moments to journal your thoughts, experiences, and visioning. What gifts does this meditation offer? What challenges does it bring? What is your life asking of you?

**Conversation Notes**: Be sure to talk with your partners, whether your marital companion or like-minded friends. How about a weekly date to get together or talk by phone? Make notes of high points in your conversations.

## Week Two Interactive Exploration

*This week we'll find ways to make the meditation a regular part of our days.*

Choose three specific times each day that will become opportunities and reminders to practice heartfulness. Even a few breaths of goodness, three times a day, to *take care of you* as you care for others. When? How about:

- when you are first conscious of being awake, in the morning; three minutes to get your self aligned, resonant, and grateful for goodness.
- when you walk the dog, take out the trash, or get the mail.
- when you help the children in the tub before bedtime

Rhythmically, day-by-day, habituate your whole being to "goodness"; you feel a small smile welling up and spreading out; you train yourself to gratitude. This lays down new neural pathways. In time, heartfulness becomes your baseline; it becomes your resting position. It is the "home" to which you return many times throughout the day.

---

**Week Two Exploration**

- Choose three times a day for Heart-breathing.
- Choose easy times to remember:
  - when you wake up?
  - while the coffee brews?
  - when waiting at a red light?
- Let heartfulness and goodness become your new default mode.
- Newsflash: you are shaping your whole brain, and therefore your whole self toward harmony.

*Write your weekly pages and talk with your partners!*

Week Three Exploration

• Deepen your practice:

  ◦ while breathing through your heart;

  ◦ while imagining a difficult situation;

  ◦ while bringing the whole situation into your peaceful heart;

  ◦ while holding and rocking the difficulty; no need to avoid or fix it;

  ◦ while imagining how things will change with the insight of your heart at play;

  ◦ while writing a word that embraces this insight; illumine it as a medieval monk might.

*Don't forget to write in your Weekly Pages, and talk with your partners!*

*Weekly Pages*

**Vision and Assessment**: Throughout the week, take a few moments to journal thoughts, experiences, and visioning: how is this "three-times-a-day" working for you? Are they the right times? Are there better times? How can you remind yourself? Can you set an alarm on your phone? How does it feel to meditate in motion? Does it help to slow down your pace a bit?

**Conversation Notes**: During your weekly partner date, ask each other these questions. Listen and encourage, but don't try to resolve the other's challenges.

## Week Three Interactive Exploration

*This week we deepen the practice to find how it can help in difficult times.*

• In addition to your regular minutes of heartfulness, add a layer of depth. This will probably need to be done in a more meditative way, during minutes when you are alone and focused:

• When you are aware that your heart rhythms have become calm and coherent, with the "eye of the heart" imagine a difficult situation that you face, perhaps with your child, at work, or at home.

• Bring this difficult situation into the coherence of your heart. Allow it to be held and rocked. Quietly observe this fact of being at peace with difficulty. Not running away. Not trying to "fix" it. If you find you are pulled into the story line, just return to the awareness of your breath moving through your heart. Let the opposites of peace and a difficult situation lie side-by-side in the coherence of your heart.

• Subtly, ask your heart if it has wisdom to offer to this situation. If the *mind* jumps in with ideas, return again to the breath in the heart. Listen to the voice of the heart; when the heart speaks, it rarely uses the word "I."

- Often the heart asks us to develop in ourselves a new quality of being, in response to a difficulty. Or to more finely tune a quality we already carry.
- Continuing with awareness of the breath in the heart, as you are rocked and held in resonance, imagine how the situation could be influenced if you bring this new quality into the interplay.
- On a blank piece of paper, write the name of the quality. Now with crayons or paint, *illuminate* your quality, the way medieval monks illuminated sacred texts. Again, put this where it can be an affirmation to you.

## Weekly Pages

**Vision and Assessment**: Throughout the week, make notes of the times this situation arises. Note the times you simply were pulled into the old dynamic. Be grateful for the times you were able to remember, even if you still remained with the old. Celebrate the times you remembered and allowed heart-resonance to influence your response!

**Conversation Notes**: Make notes of your conversations with your partners. Notice how sharing this experience with others helps you to remain conscious, even in the face of stress.

## Week Four Interactive Exploration

*This week we assess and congratulate ourselves as the practice becomes a good habit.*

- Notice how the images you created as maps, the rhythmic-throughout-the-day heartfulness practice, as well as the deepening practice of holding a difficult situation in the heart have become more intuitive: you don't have to think about them so much, don't need to give yourself instructions. Notice how they are becoming part of your life of habits. Good habits.

---

**Week Four Exploration**

- Time to assess and congratulate yourself:

  ◦ Notice that the practice is becoming intuitive.

  ◦ Think less and concentrate less as you breathe through your heart.

  ◦ Congratulate yourself! Say something good to encourage yourself.

  ◦ Talking kindly to ourselves teaches us to respond kindly to our children.

*Don't forget to write in your Weekly Pages, and talk with your partner!*

- Congratulate yourself for this. When we talk kindly to ourselves, we reinforce a positive ability to change. This is also the way we teach ourselves to speak kindly to our children.
- When we notice that we have fallen out of the heartfulness habit, with no recrimination, no self-criticism, we simply return to the goodness of the breath moving through the heart. We return to an imperceptible smile warming and spreading throughout our being. We return to resonance and harmony.

## Weekly Pages

**Vision and Assessment**: Keep a journal of the ups and downs, the remembrances, and the forgetfulness. Be aware of the words you use as you record your days. If you find frustration or derogatory words creeping in, send the breath through your heart; sigh, smile, and keep writing with goodness flowing through.

**Conversation Notes**: Share together your self-assessment of this first month. Remain aware of using nonjudgmental language. As you speak and as you listen to your partners, practice keeping an awareness of heart resonance. Make notes to refer to later.

# WEEKLY PAGES

# FAMILY LIFE RHYTHMS

Rhythm is the beginning of life itself. All life is in motion and rhythm is what brings order to this life motion. A baby in the womb has her life rhythm set by the beat of the mother's heart, her rhythmic breathing, and other synchronized body rhythms. New infants need to be kept close to the parents' hearts, because their heartbeat and breathing is not yet fully rhythmic. This close proximity "entrains" the baby's biorhythms, bringing safety and calm. Rhythmic movement brings harmony and coherence to human brainwave patterns, creating a deep sense of wellbeing and belonging. This human need for rhythm does not diminish as we grow and age; it is essential for health, happiness and a continued ability to engage fully with life, because Life is rhythm!

Therefore, *rhythm* is the magic word for parents and educators of young children. Young children thrive on a simple, flexible rhythm that carries them through their day, through each week and through the slowly unfolding years of their lives. Rhythm lays a strong foundation, not only in our children's lives but also in our own. We human beings have been shaped over the millennia by the rhythmic rotation of the earth, by the diurnal dance of day and night. Our children, who live closer to basics than we do, are affected profoundly by the life rhythms we determine for them. Not only do we want their day to be filled with rhythmic physical activities in which they can join us, such as sweeping, washing up the cups or polishing the wooden toys, but we also want these activities to move throughout the day in a rhythmic fashion. Many problems we experience with our children can be addressed by setting a simple daily rhythm that allows their needs to be met in a timely way. (from *Heaven on Earth*)

* *Rhythm* is the magic word, as we live with young children. In Section One, we began working with our inner rhythm; now let's work with outer rhythms.

* As adults, we will discover that rhythm works both from the inside out and from the outside in.

~ We all feel better when we sleep, eat, work and exercise in a rhythmic fashion (Outside-in).

~ When we are in-harmony inside, even an occasional erratic stretch can be ameliorated by our inner equanimity (Inside-out).

~ Our young children, though, do not distinguish between the inside and outside! They need us to both be in-harmony in our hearts, as well as establish for them regular daily-life rhythms. They are at-one with us and with the home-life we establish.

- Do you feel really pressured by the break-neck speed of our technological society? Here are a few reasons why:

  ◦ Many North Americans work more than forty hours a week.

  ◦ Our productivity (what is expected of us ) during those forty hours has increased by 400% since 1950!

  ◦ We produce four times the "product" than we did mid-twentieth century.

  ◦ Overwork is associated with poor health, injuries, illness and increased mortality.

  ◦ Other areas related to overwork: weight gain, increased alcohol use, increased smoking and poor neuro-psychological functioning.

- All of this pressure creates sky-rocketing stress levels. When we are stressed, our children are, too. A seven-year-old's sense of stress is this: "Stress is when I can't see my mommy or dad all day because they are working."

  ***Don't despair;
  we can beat the odds!***

How do we establish a "simple daily rhythm" when we live in a fast-pace and often frenetic society? If you are feeling pressured and stressed, here are some statistics that confirm your experience:

> "The average number of hours worked annually by workers in the United States has increased steadily over the past several decades and currently surpasses that of *Japan* and most of Western Europe."[5]
>
> It is not unusual for Americans to work more than 40 hours per week, and according to the US Bureau of Labor Statistics, the average productivity per worker has increased 400% since 1950.[6]
>
> "In a recent report by the Center for Disease Control, 'working more than 40 hours per week was associated with poorer general health, increased injury rates,. more illnesses, or increased mortality.' The Japanese language has a word for this kind of fatal pressure, *karoshi*, which translates as death-by-overwork, and Japanese corporations are now being held responsible to families of workers who die from *karoshi*."[7]

> "One meta-analysis of long work hours suggested a possible weak relationship with preterm birth. Overtime was associated with unhealthy weight gain in two studies, increased alcohol use in two of three studies, increased smoking in one of two studies, and poorer neuropsychological test performance in one study. A pattern of deteriorating performance on psycho-physiological tests as well as injuries while working long hours was observed across all study findings, particularly with very long shifts and when 12-hour shifts combined with more than 40 hours of work a week."[8]

With the continually increasing speed of our technology, there is a growing societal expectation that we try to match the lightening-pace of our technology. Clearly, from the above statistics, we see this is unhealthy and sometimes deadly. What is more difficult to see is the pain and stress that overwork creates for our children.

Asked what stress is, a child of seven answered "Stress is when I can't see my mommy or dad all day because they are working."

I think, though, that with tremendous courage and determination we can return to a more human pace. If we are willing to choose our own values, swim upstream, be questioned by friends and family, just say *no* to vast quantities of "stuff" and "busyness," our family will reap the benefits of a simple daily rhythm. Here are some ideas from *Heaven on Earth* for you to remember, dig into, and explore more deeply.

## Daily Rhythm

You can plan an open rhythm of indoor play, outdoor play, snack times, nap times, and social times with playmates. In today's society, there is pressure to give our young child "enrichment opportunities" from an exhaustive list of possibilities such as dance lessons, music lessons, and baby gymnastics. We need to remember that there is nothing more "enriching" for a young child than exploring his own world of home, filled with natural playthings and the work of caring for a family—housework, laundry, cooking—and exploring his own backyard. Look for the chapters on the magic of Indoor Play, Outdoor Play, and Artistic Experience, in *Heaven on Earth*. Here is a simple schedule you can think about and perhaps adapt to your needs:

9:00–10:30 Outdoor play. Begin the day in the fresh air!
    It sets the tone for the whole day.
10:30 Snack. Think light and simple—fruit, raisins, crackers,
    etc., and leftover tea.
11:00–12:00 Indoor play, cleanup.
12:30 Lunch, wash dishes, run outdoors a little.
1:00–3:00 Nap. Quiet time for older ones.
3:30 Snack (more on the importance of afternoon snack later).
4:00 A perfect time for a walk, or outdoor play.
5:00 Dinner preparation. Include your child!

---

• Studies show that a common thread running through well-balanced families is mealtimes. Children benefit when we share at least three meals per week together:

◦ less chance of overweight

◦ healthier diet

◦ fewer behavioral problems

◦ more likely academic success

◦ greater sense of psychological wellbeing

◦ more positive family interactions

• **Let's Just Do It!** Eat meals together! We can see clearly, from the above research, that family mealtimes nourish far more than our child's nutritional needs. Their hearts, souls and minds are fed, as well.

• When you have a hectic week coming up, plan ahead and think of three times you can eat together, whether breakfasts, snacks, or a family night out for Asian noodle-bowls.

***Bon appétit!***

*An Evening Rhythm to Try*

It is an art to let the time "flow" gracefully and to remain close to the ideal of a 7:30 bedtime!

6:00 Eat dinner
6:30 Bath time
6:50ish Out of bath, into jammies
7:00 Bedtime snack
7:10 Brush teeth; lay out clothes
7:15 Story
7:30 Candle time
Hugs and Kisses
Lights out.

**Magic bedtime snack**: Toast with honey butter and warm milk with cinnamon and honey. It works like a charm!

*About Dinnertime*

Dinnertime is a fast-disappearing tradition, and one worth saving at all costs. Dinnertime is the prime place for the handing down of culture, wisdom, language, the art of conversation, the subtleties of social relationships, and other essential human activities. It is the time when we bring our separate individual energies back together after the day. It is the place where we are knit together again as a unit, as a family. In earlier times, when the daily work revolved around the home and the surrounding land, families had more opportunities throughout the day for the handing on of values, for modeling cultural mores. Children learned life tasks at the side of their parents, at the spinning wheel or the plough. Even as recently as seventy-five years ago, farm children learned the intricacies of managing a family business in the course of their growing up, from home economics to animal husbandry to sound financial investing. Every aspect of managing a busy, diverse farm was discussed throughout the day, especially at dinnertime. This basic training in life skills continued into social picnics and church on Sunday. In our

---

**Watchword for Mealtime:
THINK**

• De-stress dinnertime by thinking ahead: make a family meal chart.

◦ Seven categories of dinners, one for each night of the week
◦ How about pasta, stir-fry, roast, soup and salad, burgers, Crock Pot, and so forth? What types and categories of food does your family like?
◦ Find three or four yummy recipes in each category. *Voilà!* You now have nearly a month of recipes, all within your own family's categories.

◦ Make your shopping list by looking at your meal chart and your recipes. Shop once a week...*what a concept!*

modern lives, as we all go off to our separate endeavors, dinnertime becomes a precious and essential time with our children.

It is tempting to make a separate early dinner of "kid food," such as macaroni and cheese, hot dogs, or tofu dogs, and then later to prepare a quiet meal for the parents to share. Occasionally, this may be just what is needed. However, if we make this a regular practice, we lose a tremendous opportunity to offer our children the best of ourselves. There is great pleasure in gathering around a table filled with lovingly prepared food and the nourishment of one another's company.

If we establish a habit of coming together at the day's end and talking with each other when our children are young, it can serve as a foundation for them as they grow through the years. Some families have a tradition of telling, each in turn, a favorite aspect of their day. For our family, this was too formal. With three boys at the table, the ceremony inevitably dissolved in gales of laughter. Instead, I would begin with a small anecdote from my day and see if I could artfully lead the conversation in a creative direction. As the children grew older, the dinner table became a place where they could voice their views and listen to adult perspectives on various aspects of life.

We have to be careful with older children to sidestep the temptation to lecture. A lecture is a sure signal to preteens to tune out. Instead we can simply share our perspective and listen respectfully to theirs. Perhaps, like many of us, they need most to speak their own thought out loud, just to hear what it sounds like. Teenagers enjoy a forum in which they can air their current feelings on everything from religion to music, finances to utopian societies.

With younger children, though, we can focus on the familiar surroundings of home and family life, the goings-on in the backyard garden, and the weather and its immediate effect on our lives— whether we needed our rain boots today or the snow will come in the night.

Dinner preparation, as with breakfast, can be simplified by thinking, shopping, and preparing a weekly plan. Try thinking of

---

**Watchword for Mealtime: *TALK***

• Dinner conversation brings huge gifts for our child!

◦ Language acquisition: your child's vocabulary will be enriched far more by sitting at a dinner table with intelligent parents, who speak using a full-range vocabulary than by years of vocabulary tests!

◦ Hearing full thoughts spoken in full sentences—in the world of info-bytes, texting and tweeting, this is crucial.

◦ Through imitation, your child learns to form full thoughts and speak full sentences.

◦ The social graces of civil conversation are one of this society's endangered species.

◦ Your child learns to listen, take in what another has said, and make a considered reply.

◦ Telling "when I was a little boy" stories at the table gives your child a new view of the long expanse of time.

seven categories of meals, such as pasta one night, Mexican another, stir-fry another, soup and toast, and so forth. If your categories are broad enough, there should be plenty of variety from week to week, yet the system remains simple and easy to manage.

You can make a beautifully decorated chart to put on your refrigerator door, so that when evening arrives after the business of the day and everyone is tired and hungry, the hard work of thinking is already complete. If you shop with the weekly round of meals in mind, then all your ingredients should be right at hand, and dinner is soon on the table. Remember to plan weekday meals that are quick to prepare. Save more complex, time-consuming dishes for weekends, when the pace is slower.

As years go by and your children develop new tastes, you will make new dinner charts. If you save the old ones in your journal, they will become a family heirloom that your grandchildren will love to pour over!

As parents, we do not know the future results of our choices and decisions about lifestyle, schooling, and spiritual direction for our children. We can only continue to educate ourselves in our decision-making and do the hard work our decisions demand. For many years to come we will be unable to see the indelible impressions we have made. We just do our best day by day and year after year in faith that our abiding love for our children will act as our guide and that love will show us the needs of each unique child of ours." (From *Heaven on Earth*)

The following is a sample meal chart you can adapt and work with. Sometimes our family made the meal chart like a circular mandala cut into seven pie wedges, which the boys then decorated. When children engage with parents in creating this rhythm, they feel an investment; they have devoted their energy to the cause. This also makes for less fuss at meal times!

Breakfasts     Dinners

| | Breakfasts | Dinners |
|---|---|---|
| Sunday | French Toast | Roast w/ Veggies |
| Monday | Oatmeal | Soup and Salad |
| Tuesday | Eggs | Mexican Casserole |
| Wednesday | Rice Cream | Burgers: veggie, beef, salmon |
| Thursday | Toaster Waffles | Pasta |
| Friday | Granola | Crock Pot |
| Saturday | Pancakes | Sea Food |

*Section Two Intention*: to delve more deeply into the specifics of family rhythms. To envision and carry through ideas to make bedtime, mealtimes, and family festivals inviting, enfolding, and nourishing. To create them with strength and flexibility. And to attend more consciously to the parent's inner rhythm (soul gesture) and outer physical rhythm through body language.

---

**Section Two Intention**

• To create family rhythms—a sense of "This is the way we do it"—during

  ◦ bedtime
  ◦ mealtimes
  ◦ family festival times

• To become more aware of parents' inner rhythm and outer physical rhythm

---

## Week One Interactive Exploration

*This week, we look carefully at Bedtime.*

- Because the quality of your child's day depends entirely upon the quality of sleep she has the night before, we'll begin our work of daily rhythms with bedtime.

- Decide on the right bedtime ritual for your family. Remember that every step you take, from the moment you call the family to dinner, is an important step toward a happy bedtime.

- When you have decided what the ritual will be, *do it the same way—every night!* Each step on the path to bed, gives your child the signal that sleep is coming soon. She will anticipate each following step and become sleepier by the moment. Smile and yawn as you walk her through the ritual...really! Smiling and yawning are both contagious human activities, so model happy sleepiness!

- You might want to try the Evening Rhythm, as above, including the magic bedtime snack. I have told hundreds of families about this snack. The only feedback I receive is how foolproof it is! Each ingredient is a natural sedative, and it guarantees that your child will not say "I'm hungry" or "I'm thirsty." More recently, I have had parents of children with food allergies tell me that gluten-free toast and warm rice milk works just as well.

*Weekly Pages*

**Vision and Assessment:** Make notes of what worked and what did not work in your bedtime ritual. Plan how you can fine-tune it. Chances are good that you have the right idea, but you and your child simply need more time adjusting. Don't give up, fine tune, and *do it the same way—every night!*

**Conversation notes:** Be sure to keep talking with your partners. Talk through the successes and challenges. Another pair of eyes can be a great help in the fine-tuning process. Write it all down, so in the busy round-of-life you don't forget!

## Week Two Interactive Exploration

*This week we focus on Mealtimes*

- As we discussed above, mealtimes are critically important for young children, so let's make them as infused with the nutrients of love as with whole foods.
- Streamline your work and minimize stress: create a weekly meal chart! Depending upon your children's ages, include them in the discussion. Make it rectangular or circular, but be sure to decorate it beautifully!
- Think simple and quick meals for weekdays and save the more labor-intensive meals for weekends. Baked foods are usually simple, because it goes into the pan and does not need attention while you prepare a salad or set the table. Ideas for quick baked foods: Chicken with potatoes, carrots, and onions in the baking dish. No boil lasagna: just layer up the uncooked noodles with the cheese and veggies and be sure to pour *plenty* of sauce on each layer. Veggie quiche in frozen crusts. Pizza in frozen crusts. Lasagna-style enchiladas—again, just layer up veggies and other things with sauce between tortillas. Check out the *Tree of Life* sample meal chart (on page 23) as a springboard for ideas and inspiration.

---

**Week One Exploration: Bedtime**

- Every step you make, from the moment dinner begins, can be an important step toward a happy bedtime.

  ◦ Decide on your family's ritual.

  ◦ Do It The Same Way Every Night!

  ◦ The repetition of each step is a signal to your child that sleep is coming.

  ◦ Try the magic bedtime snack; you will want some, too!

  ◦ Smile and yawn as you move through each phase.

  ◦ Show your child sleep is happy and desirous.

- There are so many options available for those with food allergies, you can streamline in similar ways, too.
- Put the chart on the fridge, look at it before you begin, and create the meals you have planned. This is not the time to think, "I'm not in the mood for quiche." If your child protests, simply bring him to the chart and look at it with him. Show him where it is written (in stone, so to speak). Then show him which day he *will* get to have the food he is asking for today. Delayed gratification is a great gift we give our children: it is one of the main predictors of success in life!

## Weekly Pages

**Vision and Assessment:** How did your vision for this mealtime harmony play out? How did the meal chart go? Are your categories broad enough? If your child dislikes a planned food, did you plan on something else in the menu that they do like? Now plan seven other meals, within the categories, for next week. If you roast a chicken this week, roast a butternut squash next. If you had veggie burgers this week, have salmon patties next. If you had tomato soup this week, have corn chowder next. Does this make sense to you? Stay within the category, but broaden the choices. Simple, easy, doable. Did you remember to help guide table conversation, and heart-sharing? How did that go? How was the timing? What about cleanup: one parent can begin the bedtime ritual (getting ready for bath and bathing) while the other begins cleanup.

**Conversation Notes:** Discuss with your partners how the mealtimes went. Timing, rhythm, cooperation, cleanup, beginning bedtime, and also the quality of the meals. What fine-tuning needs to happen, in any of these areas or others? Be sure to write it down! The onward rush of life can wash away the best of ideas!

---

**Week Two Exploration: Mealtimes**

- Want to streamline work and minimize stress?
  - Create a weekly meal chart.
  - Make it beautiful: you and your child can decorate it!
  - Put your chart on the fridge and just do it! This is not the moment to change your mind.
  - Don't be deterred if your child say "yuck!"
  - Simple & quick meals for weekday dinners, labor-intensive for weekends.
  - Baked and crock-pot dinners are simplest.
  - Food allergies? Don't despair: there are endless great streamlined options for you, too.

*Write your thoughts and Talk with your partners.*

# Week Three Interactive Exploration

*This week we plan a Family Festival.*

- You are probably feeling good about your family's healthy rhythms by now. Bedtime is settling into a simple ritual, and mealtimes are streamlined and going pretty well, with a hiccup here or there. Congratulations! Continue with the good effort at making these daily rhythms part of your life of habits.
- *Now is the time to look ahead to your yearly rhythms.*
- What are the festivals and celebrations your family always observes? Birthdays, a mid-winter festival of light—Hanukkah, Christmas, Solstice, Kwanzaa—Valentine's Day, a spring festival—Easter or May Day. Others, too? Make a list of the ones your family enjoys. Now, looking through, choose the particularly ones you would like to highlight.
- Look at chapter 3 in *Heaven on Earth* and reread the essential elements of a festival. Remind yourself that some elements always remain the same, and some elements need to change as the family grows and changes.
- Choose one festival you'd like to work with. Using the "Festivals" chapter as a guide, plan your celebration in advance. If you finish this, go on to the next.

## Weekly Pages

**Vision and Assessment**: This is a resting week, as you continue to enjoy the fruits of body and soul nourishing mealtimes and peaceful bedtimes. Pat yourself on the back. It is also a week to look at the "round of the year." (Make notes as you list family celebrations, choosing those to focus on…or delete.) Here, in your weekly pages, keep your detailed outline of the next one or two festivals as you envision them. You won't have to fish through file folders to find your good ideas!

**Conversation Notes**: As you talk with your partners, be sure to jot down any good ideas they may have brainstormed. Learn from

---

**Week Three Exploration: Plan a Family Festival**

- Congratulate yourself on happier bedtimes and more civilized meals! Keep going with festival plans:

  ◦ Think of stories and songs of the season.

  ◦ To decorate the house, go for a nature walk!

  ◦ Think of traditional foods.

  ◦ Prepare the festive table.

  ◦ Which elements remain the same and which need to evolve with your children's growth?

*Write your thoughts and Talk with your partners.*

**Week Four Exploration: Spotlight your inner and outer bodily rhythms**

• We have spent a good amount of time attending to the rhythms of our heart–space. Continue to allow the breath to bring goodness into your heart.

• Now let's look at our body-language: what do our gestures speak?

  ◦ Compassion and encouragement are the watch-words here!

  ◦ This is no place for self-criticism.

  ◦ Observe yourself as you go about the daily round: preparing meals, feeding the pets, sweeping, washing, cooking and more.

  ◦ Try bringing joy to the chores: rhythmic bodily movements bring harmony and peace to our nervous system. Feel the joy!

  ◦ Even if it feels phony, try smiling and sighing. Imagine feeling grateful. Science is on your side, here, so just try it!

  ◦ Doing this is part of the "outside-in" formula.

  ◦ Gratitude can be as simple as "Well, it's not as bad as it could be, and I am glad!"

*Write your thoughts and Talk with your partners.*

each other's successes as well as challenges. Be grateful to have other adults to think this through with, to ground your learning through discussion.

## Week Four Interactive Exploration

*Now we look at our own inner rhythm and outer physical rhythms.*

• As we discussed in section one, we can attend to our own inner rhythm through any form of meditation. If you have chosen Heartfulness, remember that being able to meditate with eyes open is a huge advantage for parents! So, continue throughout the day to allow the breath to move gently through your heart, to experience the goodness this brings you and your family. Be aware of the quiet smile it elicits.

• Our children are held in the daily and yearly rhythms we establish, and they are also held in the actual rhythm of our "body language," our gesture. This is a difficult practice, but see if you can become aware of, if you can make conscious, the unspoken words our bodies speak. Observe yourself with compassion and encouragement, not with criticism.

• As you prepare a meal, lay out clothing, wipe up spilled milk, feed the cat, or sweep the floor, what information is carried by your body's rhythms? Is the message that we need to finish this quickly to move on to the next thing? We need to hurry? (Or) That this particular part is distasteful, and so we do it blindly, wishing for the next thing? Try this instead:

• Bring a sense of *joy* to our daily rounds of caring activities. Moving rhythmically soothes the autonomic nervous system and engages the parasympathetic (calming and peaceful) system.

• As you wash the dining table, try large soothing circular motions. As you sweep the floor, try relaxing and making large graceful sweeps. As you wipe up a spill, try sighing, smiling, and leaning toward the task with gratitude. Sighing, smiling, and gratitude are research-based remedies that create happiness!

- I am *very* aware that there are far too many tasks required of us as we parent our children. My continual striving was trying not to hurry myself, and especially to not to hurry my children. My batting average was somewhere in the *good-enough* realm.

- A helpful practice I used at cleanup time: as I looked at the mountain of toys that had been used for grand creativity, I begin humming a little song of thankfulness to myself. I may not have felt thankful when I began, but moving slowly and rhythmically and singing to myself always worked like magic. I was always surprised to find that I felt fine and happy as the task progressed, and the children joined me not only in cleanup, but also in a healthier inner rhythm.

- This question of becoming conscious of the language of our body rhythms requires us to have *great* self-compassion and *infinite* forgiveness. Again, meditation helps not only to shape the language our bodies speak; it also helps us to observe ourselves with compassion.

- Here is a great image, used by early-childhood teachers in the Waldorf schools. As we go about our day with the children, we are like swans gliding across the lake. Full of apparent ease and beauty. But if you look below the surface, underwater you see the swan"s strong legs and feet paddling very quickly. As we paddle strongly to parent our children, let's see if we can also create times to glide.

- I'll repeat it again; the most important task is self-compassion! As you go about the daily rounds, if you remember *sometimes* to let the breath swing through the heart emanating goodness in your rhythmic gestures, it is time to congratulate yourself. It will have become second nature to you when you discover yourself silently saying to yourself statements such as "Oh, good for you!" "Well-done!" "You can do this!" Try talking to yourself in this way; you'll be surprised how helpful a little self-encouragement can be!

- Remember when we observe ourselves, that "good enough" is really good-enough. Be grateful for good-enough-ness!
- Body habits form slowly...very slowly...expect miracles, but don't hold your breath.
- When you notice that you are breathing in your heart space, or are sweeping with gratitude, celebrate this!
- Talk kindly to yourself; the self-speech center in the brain helps us navigate through life. We know we find our way better with a little kindness, with an encouraging word.

*Weekly Pages*

**Vision and Assessment:** With no self-recrimination and simply stating the facts, make notes of how this remembering of your inner rhythm went. Are there times in the day when it is easier to remember? Times that are harder? Tasks that are conducive and those that are not? Begin where your successes are and capitalize on them. If, like me, cleanup is a time when it's easy to remember body language, or maybe while washing dishes or another time, then choose this time each day to turn your attention to soothing, rhythmic body gestures. Make notes in your weekly pages, but also make a small note to yourself to pin above the toy shelf or the sink.

**Conversation Notes:** It is so helpful to have partners in this particular exercise! A listening ear is a great gift. Remember to make notes, too.

# Section Three

# FAMILY WORK

*"Work is Love Made Visible"* —KHALIL GIBRAN

A major way we show our children that we value them is in undertaking the never-ending round of "caring" activities life requires. It is not only in housekeeping and the preparation of food, in the arranging of the flow of life, but it is primarily through our *inner attitude* that we show our love. It is not just what we do; it is who we are, in the doing of the things, that speaks volumes to our children.

For example, think of all the small and large tasks involved in cleaning the house. Think of dusting, picking up each thing, rearranging. Think of sweeping, scrubbing, shining, and vacuuming. Think of fluffing the pillows, cleaning windowsills, sweeping cobwebs, digging into corners, reasserting order. Some people may think of this as drudgery, something to be completed and forgotten as quickly as possible. But there is another side, an inner side, to housekeeping. Have you noticed when you finally sit down, how each thing shines with its own particular light? Have you seen how the air sparkles with life, the rooms silently sing? I believe this shining quality is the hymn of the life force, which you, through your loving work, have brought alive. This is love made visible.

When we approach the incessant round of ordinary life-nurturing activities with an extraordinary attitude, when we understand what we are doing on a subtle level, we can free ourselves from the prevalent societal attitude that household tasks are of less value than tasks of the mind. Certainly for our young children, these tasks are essential.

- When we think of Family Work, let's keep our inner attitude in mind, as well. When we love the very this-ness of the work, we bring the scent of the sacred into the dining room as we serve the bowls of soup. Our children are nourished by the taste of love, as well as the tang of fresh herbs.
- Our children feel the love we carry for them, through this work. Invite them to join us in this "round of love"; invite them to work with us. Yes, they need to know they are loved, but they must also know they are needed; they are an integral part of the entity called "our family."

They are essential not only for furthering daily life, but also for the child's beginning understanding of the meaning of our humanity. This is work that our children can actually witness with their own eyes, unlike so much of the technological work we do. As they join us in this work, they can practice contributing toward the whole family. This prepares them to contribute, as adults, to the larger society. Our joyful attention to these tasks creates an atmosphere in which our children can grow. Our gladness in these tasks is the tilling of the soil, the weeding of the garden, the life-giving water in which their souls take root and flourish.

In earlier times, and in other cultures, tasks associated with caring for the household have been considered essential, even of sacred value. In the East, each household had a nook where the kitchen gods were honored. In some early societies it was considered a sacred duty to keep the fire alive. It was understood that in "keeping the hearth," all the essential elements of life come into play, and through their alchemical mingling, something new is born, a transformation occurs.

Perhaps the place in the home in which all of these elements come into play the most often is the kitchen. All of the transformative activities of cooking, eating, cleaning, conversation, and laughter take place in this central area. Is this the reason why the kitchen is often the best-loved room in the house? It is the room most filled with the rich tapestry of life force, with all these elements weaving together to make our family's culture palpable.

In past times, people knew that there was tremendous power in working with the elements, these building blocks that give form to the world—and that the alchemical interaction of the physical elements and their more subtle corollaries even shaped the human soul. They understood that in the keeping of the hearth also lived the keeping of the heart, and therefore the keeping of the whole society. (from *Heaven on Earth*)

It is essential that our children know we love them, but they must also know that *we need them!* So, ask them to join us in the work. And keep the work rhythmic!

## *Have the Children Join You!*

Children live in the rhythms of their bodies more than we adults do. We can help bring a sensory experience of rhythm into their lives through daily rhythmic tasks. When we awaken each morning, we can ask their help in stirring the herbal tea, or in setting out bowls and spooning the oatmeal. They can help with their small broom as we sweep after the meal. Because they learn by imitation, it will help the development of their natural "whole-body" awareness if we bring greater consciousness to our own gestures as we go about these daily activities. As we wash the morning dishes, sweep the floor, dust the furniture, let's ask ourselves what our child sees in our gesture. Does he see care in our bodily rhythm as we bend toward the task, or does he see a hurried duty? Does he see our pleasure in the task, or resentment? Because the young child learns by imitation, he will imitate not only our physical gestures, but also our "inner gesture." We can teach our child to enjoy the rhythmic activity of the care of his toys and playthings by our own conscious enjoyment of the care of our home. As we bring our conscious presence to the rhythm of these tasks, we give our child a dual gift: a sense of purpose and presence in the rhythms of daily life.

Many of our routine tasks have been relegated to the domain of machines: vacuum, washing machine, coffee grinder, orange juicer, bread machine, and more! Let's ask ourselves which of these tasks must be done by machine, and which ones we can still do by hand. The tasks we do with our young child by hand will be the ones they know by heart when they are grown. If we feel the dishes must be done by machine, can we save the cups to do by hand? Can we offer our child a basin of warm soapy water and a sense of purposeful work? Once a week, could we wash the place mats from the kitchen table by hand? Vacuuming may be necessary on a weekly basis, but

---

• Of course, we need our machines of convenience. But be sure there is plenty of "hand-work" for our children to join.

◦ Save some cups or bowls out of the dishwasher to be washed at a little table by hand.

◦ Save the vacuuming for after their bedtime; instead you can sweep with a big broom and they sweep with a small one.

◦ Have the family use rakes, large and small, and save the leaf-blower for when they have a play-date.

◦ Rhythmic body-movements engage the para-sympathetic nervous system: we are calmed, regenerated, and healed from the inside out!

*Just do it! You'll love it!*

daily we can sweep with a broom, our child following along with a child-size broom. Or we can give our child the task of "sweeping" the carpet with one of the old-fashioned, nonelectric carpet sweepers that are still carried in many department stores. This is a task that four- to six-year-olds love! Certainly our lives are busy with all the pressures of career, finances, and so forth, but if we look carefully at the course of each day and comb through the events of the week, we will find small tasks that we can do by hand with our young child.

It may help you remember these "hand tasks" if you organize them on a daily and weekly basis. Some tasks, like washing the cups, need to be done daily. Others, like polishing the wood furniture and a few of your child's wooden toys as well, can be done on a weekly basis.

By participating in the "hand work" of caring for the home, our child learns, in a rhythmic, physical way, to love and care for the materiality of this earth. When we share with our children these whole-body tasks, we model for them a total, integrated gesture. By imitating us, they learn purposeful movement and how to use the body in efficient, graceful ways. We can rake leaves, shovel snow, turn the soil in the garden; we can wash windows, dust with a feather duster, polish wooden furniture. This is a great "home remedy" for the effects of media images of erratic, harried, and hurried movement. We only have to tune our eyes and our hearts to look for the small, significant opportunities to bring a sense of bodily rhythm into our children's lives."

## A Simple Family Work Day Plan

You will find ways to share tasks that will work for your family. Here is one way to think through the chores and accomplish them in one day. There are four major indoor jobs:

- dusting and vacuuming
- laundry
- cleaning the kitchen
- cleaning the bathroom

Let us assume there are two adults sharing these tasks, and each parent will focus on specific areas. The person who dusts and vacuums will have more flexibility, and so can be putting loads of laundry through the washer and dryer. The parent who does kitchen and bathroom is more involved with water and scrubbing, so needs more concentrated energy. When our young children are working alongside us, we will want to give attention to their "soundscape." So we can send them off to help with the kitchen, after the dusting and shining is finished, while the vacuum is being run. Usually, in the average house, these tasks can be finished in two or three hours, even with our children underfoot and helping.

You can then have a good, quick lunch together, perhaps sandwiches, or leftovers. Afterward, while one parent does outdoor work and the children play in the yard, the other parent can shop for groceries. This will be easy—look at the chart of daily dinners and make the shopping list with this visual aid. Back at home, the children will go down for a nap mid-afternoon. By day's end you will have a sparkling house, a full refrigerator, clean laundry for the week, and happy children who by joining you have learned the joy of caring for life. Because you have planned well, your energy will be wisely spent, and you will be prepared for the week to come.

To some people, all this planning may look like a form of slavery! In fact, it is through planning wisely that we actually make space for the open-ended and creative aspects of our life together. When all the necessary chores are planned into the ongoing rhythm of the day and the week, we make space available for unexpected spontaneity. We have created time to listen to the surprising insights, theories, and questions our children offer and time to imaginatively respond. We give ourselves the time to watch the butterfly with our four-year-old.

As our children grow and mature, their household tasks can evolve as well. Various chores we have shared can become their own responsibility. Of course, for many years they will not share responsibility equally, yet it is essential for their self-esteem to feel that their help and input is not only respected, but *needed* as well. As

> **All this planning of bedtimes, mealtimes, festivals, and workdays creates huge freedom of mind! How? With repetition, these "ways of life" become simple habits, healthy and life affirming. No more fret and stress of wondering "What is next?" or "How do I approach it today?" The answer lives in our bones!**

our children reach school age, around six or seven, we can give them daily and weekly chores. We can give the care of a family pet to our six- or seven-year-old, incorporating feeding the cat into the evening routine, perhaps as soon as dinner is finished. Or we can include setting the dinner table, or laying out his clothes the night before.

The key is to attach this new responsibility onto a part of his day that is already very well incorporated. We can add a new action onto what is already a well-known habit. The attitude we can carry, as we give our children more responsibility little by little, is, "You are a member of our family and we need you, in many ways, for warmth and fun, for work and play." Eventually, when our children become teenagers, we can give them various tasks to envision and accomplish on their own. Teenagers love to grocery shop, and although they may not be as thorough or economical as we are, their shopping is full of adventure and surprises. We can give them one night a week in which they are responsible for preparing the family meal. Although they may need some coaching at first, they will know many aspects of cooking, having stood on a chair beside us for so many years as we have chopped and stirred." (from *Heaven on Earth*)

*Section Three Intention*: to help parents actualize the knowledge that our children must know that we *need* them. To organize plans for daily work chores: daily toy tidying, a weekly family workday, and understanding the necessity of decluttering.

## Week One Interactive Exploration

*This week we plan and actualize a daily chore plan.*

- Let's prepare a daily work-chore plan. You can think through the necessary work at different times of day, and think of ways to incorporate your child. Often, small acts of love arrive in the form of work!

- Remember that chores are age-specific: for example at breakfast, your three-year-old can put a spoon beside each bowl.

Your four-year-old can put out the bowls and spoons. Your six-year-old can set the table. Look at your meal chart on the fridge and decide age-appropriate breakfast chores.

- If you and your child are at home during the days, she can join you in watering plants, sweeping the porch, kneading bread dough and such. If your family is gone most days, these chores can be incorporated into the family workday on the weekend.

- Think through the late afternoon/evening tasks. Again, look at your meal chart, and find ways they can *age-specifically* help to prepare the dinner; can they cut a small carrot spear as you chop close beside them? A few years later, can they prepare the whole salad? Can they place olive slices on the top of the pizza? Can an older sibling watch the timer and take the pizza out of the oven? After dinner, can they wash their little cup and plate in a basin of warm water? A few years from now, can they rinse plates and fill the dishwasher?

- You get the idea: break the many tasks of the daily workload into small increments and choose their chores wisely.

- The Golden Rule: Children Learn by Imitation, so *do your chores in their presence.* Many hands make light work, and many hands working together bring joy!

**Week One Exploration:**

Make a daily Chore Chart:

- Make the chores age-specific.
- Think of daily breakfast chores.
- Think of plant and animal care chores
- Think of daily dinner chores.
- The Golden Rule: do your chores in their presence! Imitation reigns supreme.

*Write your thoughts and Talk with your partners.*

## Weekly Pages

**Vision and Assessment:** Are you beginning to get a feel for the joy working together as a family brings? Remember to focus not only on the fact of the chores, but the inner experience of subtly weaving your family's energy together through work. How can you fine-tune the mornings? Evenings? Do you need to adjust the chores to become more age-appropriate? Your child wants a challenge, so give a chore that takes some concentration. If it's not something breakable, you might make the chore just a tiny bit beyond her current capacity.

**Conversation Notes:** Write down your thoughts and ruminations with your partners. You know how daily life can erase the best ideas!

## Week Two Interactive Exploration

*This week we'll discover the wonder of the "sorting basket."*

- This week, let's take a break from this focus on work and introduce *magic* into the daily rounds! I'm talking, of course, about a little piece of magic in the midst of tidying the toys. If your children are as creative and vigorous at fort-building as my boys were, when you look at the house after a day full of adventure and fun—the couch cushions (and every pillow in the house) commandeered for domiciles, the dining chairs tied together stretching the length of the living room, and every toy on the shelf having been an essential element in The Game— you know that only magic will get you through.

- Yes, I am talking about the magic of Heartfulness, but also about another piece of functional magic: the toy-sorting basket.

- Go to the store and buy an old-fashioned, oval-shaped, reed laundry basket with an opening at either end as a handle.

- At cleanup time, until your children are grade-school age and even in the second or third grade, they will need your help if they have really thrown their hearts and all the toys into their creativity.

- About five to ten minutes before you need their help, get the sorting basket and begin to gather up the unused toys, giving a little information announcement: "Finish up your game, now. I am going to need your help in a few minutes." They may protest that the toys are going away, but assure them that you are only taking the ones they are finished with.

- Put the small abandoned toys in the sorting basket—the knit barn animals, small wooden trucks, conch shells, wooden blocks, and such.

- I call this the "under-cleaning." When the toys are no longer underfoot and are in the sorting basket(s), begin to dismantle the parts of the forts that have been abandoned. Continue to remind them to finish the game. Usually this works, but if not, at some point say "We're all finished playing now. I need your help" Usually the big-energy work of untying furniture and returning it to its proper place is a good incentive for them to allow play to flow into work.

- When all the furniture is in place, now enters the magic of the sorting basket: because you have done the under-cleaning, the room already looks clean! I think children abhor cleanup for the same reason we do: everything looks so messy and impossible.

- The basket sits in the center of the room, and the children go to the basket, choose a toy that is *on the top of the pile,* and return it to its proper place on the toy shelf. This part goes lickety-split because the floor is cleared and it's easy to get to the toy shelf. No tripping over the toys on the way.

- Just try this, and you'll be amazed! Early Childhood teachers who have incorporated this into their classroom have a simple orderly, cooperative cleanup experience, and so can you!

## *Weekly Pages*

**Vision and Assessment**: This is another week to sit back and relax. The real magic of the sorting basket should be helping your overall experience of Family Work. Take time to journal not just about toy tidying, but also your general sense of how working together as a family is progressing.

**Conversation Notes**: Enjoy sharing your experience of the ease of toy cleanup with your partners. Take a moment to look back over the fruits of a regular, rhythmic family life and the "visible love" that family work is. Make notes for the future.

## Week Three Interactive Exploration

*This week, we can explore creating a weekly family work day.*

- In the introductory thoughts, I offered "A Simple Work Day Plan" that involves dividing tasks into four categories (with each

**Week Three Exploration**

Make a Workday plan:

⋄ One parent works with the children at dusting, vacuuming and laundry.

⋄ The other parent concentrates on the kitchen and bathroom; small helpers will love these chores. They seem more like water play than work.

⋄ Your adolescents may not love this, but they need to be required. They need these skills to walk , well-equipped, into the world!

⋄ Do the above chores in the morning, then have a healthy quick lunch.

⋄ In the afternoon, one parent stays with the children and does outdoors chores, while the other grocery shops. This is easy: look at your weekly meal chart and make the shopping list with this help.

*Write your thoughts and Talk with your partners.*

parent taking care of two of them) and innovating ideas to incorporate your children. Think through the weekly work that needs to be done at your house and see if you can categorize or organize them into an equal amounts of time spent for each parent. Be sure to include the extra time involving help from small hands.

• In the dusting and vacuuming category, a chore I loved as a child was to polish the baseboards. I was small and loved to crawl along behind the furniture and drapes, and to get into all the little interesting corners. It gave me good ideas for new fort-building endeavors, as well as hide-and-seek advantages. I never found dusting as interesting as polishing, so my brother dusted ahead of me, and I polished away in the rear. Sweeping with a broom was too complicated, but a small hand broom and dustpan were perfect for under the dining table and, again, the corners.

• Try to remember being as small as your child and think of cleaning chores that are similar to play. Allow your children to play at their work. For them work and play are undifferentiated.

• As you did for the Meal Chart, make a Chore Chart for the fridge. Again, be sure to give your child the opportunity to invest by having him help with decorating it beautifully.

• About praise and criticism: It is tempting to over-praise or criticize as our children work beside us. We can train ourselves simply to say verbally what we notice about their actual work. Something like, "When you push the sponge down hard like that, see how it makes the jelly drip stain go right away." "When you sweep the corners, try holding the broom in this hand, and the dustpan in the other…see how it picks up the crumbs better."

• When the whole family is working together, there is less a temptation to hurry through grumpily. It is an invitation to enjoy the rhythmic activities, to enjoy each one's presence and to enjoy the tapestry of your work together. As the children grow, be sure to give them chores that are challenges, just a little beyond their reach.

*Weekly Pages*

**Vision and Assessment:** Plan your workday and *do it*. Notice as you work together where the glitches are, which chore works for a small helper and which doesn't. In addition, notice which chores are temperamentally suited best for each family member. Make notes and refine the process for next week. Keep working and refining until it feels like a well-greased wheel that rolls along smoothly.

**Conversation Notes:** Stay in touch with your partners as the weeks go by. Another pair of eyes and another perspective is invaluable.

## Week Four Interactive Exploration

*This week, we work with substructure.*

- This week, we will tackle the substructure beneath family work: decluttering, lightening the load, trimming down the "stuff"
- Kim Jon Payne's book *Simplicity Parenting* offers a wonderful rationale for paring down and thinning out the "stuff" in our family's life. I recommend buying it today, if you don't already own it.
- You will decide for yourself which room in the house is the best place to begin. I would recommend that you *not* begin with your child's toy shelf! Begin in the kitchen or your office; allow your child to witness the process of decluttering.
- This process will take much longer than a week, but this week is a good time to begin!
- In the kitchen, gather all the leftover containers that you never use, the food processor from the 1980s that your mom gave you and you haven't touched, all the extra spatulas, slotted spoons, and the rusty meat fork. Have your child help you put them in a box. On Family Work Day, he can help grocery shop and then drop the giveaway box at the second-hand store.

---

**Week Four Exploration**

Now we de-clutter:

- Decide which room to begin with: Kitchen? Office?
- Let your child join the process of filling boxes.
- Take him to the second-hand store, to give away the boxes.
- What's next? Books and magazines next?
- When it's time to do his room, it will be a familiar process.
- If he's old enough he might like to help choose what to give away.
- At dinnertime talk about the wonderful feeling of lightening the load!

*Write your thoughts and Talk with your partners.*

- Do the same thing with your books and magazines; your child can help drop them at the library. The same for your office and the paper recycle bin.
- When it is time to declutter your child's room and toy shelf, it will all seem like part of the process of family work. Depending upon his age, he can help choose which toys he has outgrown and might now be needed by a younger child. Same with clothing. If you know a family with a younger child, this makes it more personal and satisfying. If not, Goodwill is ready and waiting.
- If your child protests strongly about a particular toy or piece of clothing, you can say something like "Oh, if you are not ready to give it away yet, that is fine. We can wait a while."
- Discuss this with each other, maybe at dinnertime, how great it feels to pass along the things in your life that are no longer helpful and needed. Model for her the sense that materiality is always passing through—helping us when we need it and then moving on to help someone else.

*Weekly Pages*

**Vision and Assessment:** How *does* decluttering feel to you? Write about it, perhaps make a poem, or even draw a picture of the felt-experience. Record this feeling, so next year, when you are dreading decluttering time, you'll have an incentive to *just do it*!

**Conversation notes:** How do your partners feel about this? Compare notes. Decide to give each other pep talks when it comes 'round next time. Enjoy the feeling of lightness and space together!

# WEEKLY PAGES

## Section Four

# FAMILY PLAY

Let's return to the image of family culture as a family's container, to hold and foster the children's growth. The structured, rhythmic completion of weekly housework can be balanced by the spaciousness and freedom of the family's play together. In the same way we considered having one day per week as a workday, we may want to choose one day for family outings. Again, you will find a rhythm of playing together that is right for your family.

For our young children, play is a way of life, and so providing opportunities to play together can be a simple matter of going outdoors together. We adults can sit and chat as we swing the children on the high seas of the hammock, or we can putter together in the garden as the children play close by. For young children, an occasional "tag" or "chase" game is fine fun with Mom and Dad. Hide and seek is sweetly poignant, as our young children call out from six feet away, "You can't find me!" Remember, though, if we enter too deeply into their magical realm with all of our adult thoughts and energy, we can actually disturb their world of play.

When our children reach grade-school age, though, they have entered a new realm, and we can join them in games that involve rules and sequencing. In the appendix you will find resource books mentioned that introduce noncompetitive, physically active games that can be played by a few players or by many. Maybe you will ask another family over for an afternoon of outdoor games! Look for games that value all players, regardless of their varying ability levels. We can also choose games that call for specific qualities, such as quickness or solidity. This gives each player, regardless of capacity, his or her moment in the sun. It is marvelous for children

- Playing together balances working together.
- Family Play with little children can be simple: go outdoors!
  - Swing together in the hammock.
  - Putter as you weed.
  - Nibble early lettuces.
  - Rake a pile of leaves and jump in.
- Save games with rules and sequencing for the grade-school years. Check out the New Games books and the New Games Foundation. *Noncompetitive* is the watchword, here.
- Wait till adolescence for competitive sports games. Introduced too early, they can
  - Restrict free-movement and the whole-body/heart/mind development this creates
  - Hamper creative problem-solving and social inclusion
  - Encourage specific muscle-group usage to the detriment of broad-spectrum usage

to see their parents in a completely different role, running, hiding, falling, sliding!

We can save competitive sports games for later, when our children are near adolescence. Introduced too early, these games can restrict not only free movement, but also creative problem solving and a sense of social inclusiveness. Sports games can also negatively affect our young children's balanced physical development, encouraging the repetitive use of specific muscle groups to the neglect of others, and encouraging specific ball-oriented eye–hand usage to the detriment of a more age-appropriate, broad-spectrum usage. At adolescence, though, when the physical development is nearly complete, competitive sports games can be introduced. Sportsman-like coaching is essential in teaching the value of the opponent and brisk competition as one avenue to further personal excellence.

Another way we can bring play into our family culture is to discover what it is that we really like to do all together as a family. If we love water, we can move along a developmental waterway, so to speak, bringing to our family developmentally appropriate water activities. With our preschool children, we can take a camping trip beside a river, stopping at a spot where the water runs wide and slow. This way our little ones can potter along ankle-deep, discovering crayfish and minnows, water-skaters and salamanders. In a few years, we'll be looking for good swimming holes. Eventually canoes and boating may enter the picture, and our teenagers may vote for a whitewater rafting trip. Or, if we like to walk together, we can begin with strolls through the city park system, moving on to country hikes on trails redesigned from old railway beds, then to mountain backpacking trips. Maybe we like wheels, beginning with a tricycle ride down the sidewalk and ending many years later in a bicycle tour of France.

We will want to attend to several considerations: we need to see that our family's play is an active exploration of our beautiful planet, that it affords opportunities to discover each other as we grow and develop, and that each person finds something to love in our joined activities. One way our family played together was through ski vacations. All the men of the family loved to throw themselves against the elements and the mountain. I, on the other hand, loved to get them up, breakfasted, and off to the slopes. Then I had hours of solitude and silence, to read or walk in the snow, until mealtime rolled around and they arrived back, happily starving. Let's plan play into our daily, weekly, and yearly life. Our playing together is a colorful ribbon woven into the fabric of our family's culture." (from *Heaven on Earth*)

## Noncompetitive Game Ideas

There are wonderful resources for noncompetitive games! The *New Games* books[9] are full of fun games for all ages of children. Borrow a copy from your library or invest in one for your family. It will be a treasure you will return to again and again. Here are a few ideas I have collected from parents and friends over the years. Some are for children kindergarten or grade-school age; they may be too vigorous for smaller children.

- Socks Off: For this game, everyone has to be wearing socks (but not tights) and no shoes. They all get down on their hands and knees, and the aim of the game is to remove everyone else's socks while not letting yours come off. If your socks are pulled off, you're not out but you just keep on going. The game ends when everyone is barefoot.

- Blanket Toss: Get a large blanket and put a selection of soft toys in it. This really does mean soft all over so watch out for any teddies with hard plastic noses. Everyone grabs an edge or corner of the blanket and shakes it to make the soft toys fly up in the air. The game ends when all the toys have flown off the blanket and/or everyone's exhausted. A variation can be played with balloons, although these fly off more readily, so might be better for younger children.

- Bring our children into the activities that we love to do:
  - Play in water?
  - Love the outdoors?
  - Hooked on hiking?
  - How about biking?
- Think into the future;
  - How will this family evolve through the years?

- Obstacle Courses: Use chairs, tables, blankets, large boxes, beanbags, and the like to create an obstacle course. Children take turns at negotiating their way up, around, over, through, and under the obstacles. On a hot day, if the children are dressed appropriately for it, one obstacle could be a lawn sprinkler that has to be jumped or stepped over.

- Treasure Hunts: Start with a clue that takes you to a new location, where you'll find another clue and so on until you get to the final destination where there is a stash of treasure to be shared. Keep the number of clues and the difficulty of them age-appropriate. For pre-readers, draw pictures of each location, indoors or out!

- Sardines (an oldie but goodie): This is sort of reverse hide and seek, where the person who's "it" goes off and hides somewhere (establish out of bounds areas first to make sure nobody hides in the dog kennel or in your office closet where the computer cords are kept). Now, count out loud to twenty or thirty before the other players go and hunt for the person who's "it." When someone finds the person who's "it," they hide with them behind the curtain or under the couch or wherever. This continues until the last person comes along and finds everyone giggling. The last person to find the hiding place is "it" for the next round.

- Musical Dress-ups: Put a whole lot of dressing up clothes and props in a big bag. Set up cushions as if for musical chairs/cushions. Everyone dances while the music plays, but when the music stops, everyone sits down on a cushion. The person sitting on the designated "magic cushion" gets to reach into the bag of dress-ups and pull something out. They then put this item on and the game continues. Change the magic cushion from time to time and make sure that everyone gets a roughly even number of dress-up items to wear. When everyone is dressed, dance together with the music.

*Section Four Intention*: To help parents know the importance of playing together as a family. To show parents ways to model playfulness, with their children. To help parents bring Family Play into their daily, weekly, and yearly rhythms and to offer ideas for play in each of these areas.

## *Week One Interactive Exploration*

*This will be a fun week: let's look at playfulness with our children on a daily and weekly basis.*

- To join our children in a little bit of play on a daily basis is wonderful and invigorating for the whole family! With your very young child, to *gallop* together like ponies as you go get the mail is good fun; then hop back like bunnies. After bath, while in fresh jammies, you can "log roll" on the living room carpet with them. This brings giggles, and also gets the last of the wiggles out, before bedtime.

- The game my boys loved best to play with me, when they were in the lower grades, was to pillow-fight. I was fine with three against one, until the day a few years later that they got me down so I couldn't get up and then they tickled me! They were elated, but after that, I was only willing to go one-on-one, to their great regret.

- If you choose to designate one weekend day to work together, plan another day, or the afternoon of the same day, to play together.

- As mentioned in the introductory thoughts, think through what activities you really love to do, then adapt a way to incorporate the whole family on a weekly basis. Think toward the future, as you are planning. What activities can grow with the family, as it grows? What will offer continuing challenges over the years?

---

**Section Four Intention:**

• To know the importance of family play as well as how to model playfulness. To plan Family Play into daily, weekly, and yearly rhythms.

**Week One Exploration**

• Think of ways to be playful in the course of the day: take giant steps together to the bathroom, take baby steps back. Pick up the dropped toy with your toes. Fly together like birds as you head outdoors...

• Plan a weekly family play day. Be sure the activities are active, inclusive, nature-oriented and fun for all.

*Write your thoughts and Talk with your partners.*

*Weekly Pages*

**Vision and Assessment:** How did you find ways to bring playfulness into your daily life? Were you able to make this age-appropriate? Sometimes adults can get enthusiastic about our own fun during playfulness, that we lose track of our children's responses. We can tell the age-appropriateness by looking inquiringly into our child's eyes. If our child is delighted, there will be softness in the eyes amid the laughter. If the game is a little too rough or boisterous, we can see a wariness or reticence, even if they are laughing. So, keep eye contact steady and adapt the pace to our child's comfort level.

How did a family play day evolve? Was it a good choice of activity? Was there a way for everyone to be involved? Was there plenty of laughter and a sense of being centered and grounded? What needs to be fine-tuned for next week? What needs to be expanded? Staying in touch with each one's response keeps the playfulness alive.

**Conversation Notes:** Make notes of yours and your partners' ideas, areas that worked and those that need attention.

## Week Two Interactive Exploration

*This week we explore yearly play vacations.*

- Let's being to think about how to incorporate play into your family's yearly rhythm. Is one of your family play day activities something that can be expanded into a yearly outing?
- Our family loved to swim, and so we spent many long, long summer days at the little pond just down the road. Because of this love of water, we took a beach vacation each year. Although there were plenty of distractions—bumper cars and water slides, restaurants and movies—our vacation consisted of going to the beach right after breakfast. Hours later we came back for lunch and naps. As the boys grew older, we played games together at our beach house in the heat of the day. Then we made another return to the beach later in the afternoon. After a late dinner at

---

**Week Two Exploration**

- Plan a yearly holiday that involves active play! Can one of your weekly play day activities grow into a yearly holiday?
- Don't let the mega-marketers commandeer your family's attention! Plan your play in line with your own values and in your own competent hands.

*Write your thoughts and Talk with your partners.*

home, we returned to the beach again with flashlights to search for hermit crabs and other exciting treasures. Eventually surfing, kayaking, and other water sports evolved, to meet growing capacities and interests.

• You can see how it can be, if you choose your family play vacation well, that you do not need to be overwhelmed by the commercial culture. There is a multi-billion dollar industry committed to assure you that your family *needs its assistance* to have fun! But I know you can do it your own way, with your own intelligence and ingenuity.

• As you choose your yearly play outing, be sure there is something fun for each member of the family. If one member of the family is less enthused than others are, brainstorm ways for her to have a great time, too. If we begin this tradition when the children are young, though, chances are very good that everyone will love whatever you have chosen, simply because of the nourishment of being together in a playful way.

## Weekly Pages

**Vision and Assessment:** Write down what your vision of this holiday will be. Write your intentions, and wishes. Write your hopes and fears. Begin to create your yearly play outing in your mind's eye, and watch it grow as your family grows. This is how we create new traditions.

**Conversation Notes:** Show each other your ideas from the visioning and assessing work. Allow the synchrony of yours and your partners' ideas to play together; see what emerges!

WEEKLY PAGES

# CHILDREN'S ARTISTIC EXPERIENCE

Artistic expression is an essential element of a balanced "diet" of experience for our young children. In artistic work, we accomplish two essential tasks of childhood: the training of the hand and the training of the heart. Together these lay a firm foundation for the training of the mind.

I wrote this in a summer journal as I watched the children modeling natural clay, with total absorption, at the stream bank:

> I see their hands move lively and quick. Unconsciously they live the gift of an opposable thumb. Today I am thinking of our ancestors, all the way back to the cave, and the central place of the hand. In every culture, until perhaps the last forty years, hand-education has been an integral part of growing up. Hands were taught to carve stone arrowheads, to weave baskets, to mold clay pots, to hunt, to cure, to cook, to spin and weave, to sow and harvest. What are hands taught in the twenty-first century? At what expense do their hands lie limp in their laps? As their hands languish unused, so follow their minds. How can we measure the impact of a well-coordinated, steady, finely tuned hand? What riches does this hand bring into their life? What do these well-trained hands have to offer the world?

Neurologist Frank Wilson shows us in his book *The Hand: How It Shapes the Brain, Language, and Culture* the pivotal place of the human hand, equipped with our amazing thumb, in the evolution of the species. He argues passionately for the education of the hand, assuring us that people who use their hands, woodworkers, artists and plumbers alike, have a way of knowing the world that is inaccessible to those who have less hand training. We know that the density of nerve endings in our fingertips is enormous, and when

- Art trains your child's hands and at the same time tunes her heart! These lay a firm foundation for the development of the mind.

- Artistic activities are tools for the development of the Self. Through your child's feeling response to color, form, texture, and such, he also discovers subtle layers of himself.

- He makes relationship to the world as he "speaks" through his art.

these are engaged in childhood, the brain is enriched beyond measure. Through artistic expression, the hand, and therefore the mind, is introduced to its own astonishing creative potential.

The heart, too, is cultivated through the arts. As we look at the various artistic media, let us remain aware that the child explores not only color, form, texture, density, elasticity, and so forth. Through the physicality of this exploration, the child discovers her own self. Each of these avenues of expression elicits a feeling response from the child. In this way the child, who in early childhood does not differentiate herself from the world, begins to experience parameters that in time will become an "I." Through art, the seed of self is watered and nurtured.

The young child also makes relationship with the world through art. Children come to us from other realms, "trailing clouds of glory," as Wordsworth says. Through all their multifaceted experience, they begin to know this world of density and form. It is surely through the focused intention we parents bring, in the shape of artistic experience, that they find rich ways to reply to what the world speaks to them: they learn to make relationship.

*To explore the self and to love the world—this "heart-knowing" is learned by hand.*

### Beeswax Crayoning

How do we understand the great proliferation of our children's drawings? Filled with color and movement, what are they telling us? If we understand them properly, we can see them as icons along the course of our child's developing consciousness. The first "drawings" our child will offer us, as a toddler, are the simple tracings of movement. A child of this age is compelled to discover her environment, and thereby herself, through movement. The first drawings we see trace this exploratory path. The toddler's consciousness is the movement itself, and this is what we see on the page. Put the paper in front of her and a crayon in her hand. Her hand is already always in motion, and now this new object, the crayon, makes her movement visible to her. Remarkable!

Soon she learns that the brightly colored thing consistently obeys as her hand moves back and forth. There will be much repetition of this tracing of movement, which makes its own developmental journey. At first we will see light strokes of color, a few tentative marks on the page. Then, with repetition and the development of eye–hand coordination, the strokes become stronger.

You can encourage this experience by joining your child in crayoning. Simply lay color down on the page, with delight and attention. Move the crayon in your hand back and forth, back and forth. As with painting, at this early stage, do not be tempted to create form. Wait until your child shows you her own beginnings of form.

Allow yourself to enjoy the color as it emerges on the page, simply for its own sake. Choose different colors and lay them down together, side by side. Play with them. Your interest and enjoyment will draw your child more fully into her own experience. If she puts a few strokes of color on the page and says, "I'm finished," you can reply, "Here's a beautiful purple for you, and here's one for me. Let's color purple." A very young child will want to hop up in a minute or two, but you can coax her to stay a bit longer, saying,

"I'm going to make all my white paper shine with color." Eventually, she'll stay longer, and with a stronger capacity for will, her paper will shine with color, too.

Sooner or later, this tracing of movement will begin to form a circle. Your child may practice for a long time, repeating the mystery, discovering again and again how a line can manage to find its way home, right back where it started. One magic day, you'll discover two little dots in the circle, and your child will say, "It's me!" Or, "It's you!" This portrait making begins with the human face, a circle with two dots for eyes, and maybe a dash for the mouth. You will notice that usually the arms and legs sprout right out of the head. These limbs can be very disproportional, long, and tentacle-like. The child is showing us pictorially how critical it is that he explore his world with these fabulous powerful tools, his arms and legs.

The formation of a trunk with limbs attached often waits until the child is close to five, and we may wait a while longer for the

> Your child's drawings trace a developmental sequence beginning with simple strokes of color on the page.
>
> ◦ This slowly shifts, becoming a circle, then a face, limbs sprout from this happy little head. Later a trunk emerges as head and limbs become more proportional.
>
> ◦ Each of these stages represents a subtle shift in her consciousness.
>
> ◦ Her figure will probably float through space filled with rainbows, stars and flowers for a period of time.
>
> ◦ Finally, as she moves toward grade-school readiness, her people descend to earth, standing firmly upon the ground. Ground below, heavens above and a happy little soul smiling from the page!

limbs to come into proportion. Now the central figure begins to be attended by many supporting shapes. Trees, birds, clouds, rainbows—or, along another track, backhoes, boats, trains—all these figures dance merrily across the page. Frequently they "float" in space together, gloriously disproportional and more indicative of the child's interests than of the actual object. They can remind us of the splendid joy in life we see in ancient cave paintings, filled with vigor and innocent wisdom.

Sometime around the age of six (remember, these ages are approximate) these figures become grounded. Terra firma appears at the bottom of the page, and the arch of blue sky soars above. The central figure walks with feet firmly planted on the earth, and by now the arms and legs are more proportional. Attending figures tend to be bilateral, that is, evenly placed on either side of the central one. Harmony and balance reign.

We can see every child's drawing as a self-portrait, showing us where she stands upon a natural developmental path. One of the markers we can look for in determining when our child is ready for academic work and grade school is the appearance of this grounded little person, who no longer flies through the air with the rainbows, but walks upon the earth with rest of us.

Another artistic path your child's drawings might take is a non-representational, geometric progression. Rather than figures, your child might be drawn to the purity of shape and color. As with the progression along the representational path, your child may be drawn at an earlier stage simply to color shapes that randomly fill the page with riotous color.

In time, this shape making begins to have a relationship to the page, and you may see your child draw a large central cross on the page, thereby quartering it. The cross is a universal symbol used by most ancient peoples. It is a symbol of the self, the "I," as it emerges from the mists. This quartering can grow into graphs, the page filled with horizontal and vertical lines. Encourage her not only to create the graph, but to decorate the interior spaces with color.

You will see this graph making become more precise, and by about age five, the lines move toward a diagonal. The corners of the page may be colored diagonally and move, like a "god's eye weaving," toward a central focus.

Look for the day your child draws, not a cross, which is an earlier developmental stage, but an "X" from corner to corner. Vibrant color decorates this new stage. This capacity to envision and create a cross-lateral form is an indication of a specific stage of brain development. The child simply cannot do this task until the brain grows into this stage.

The Brain Gym system works with helping children with sensory integration problems accomplish exactly this, cross-laterality, as well as many other "brain calisthenics." I play a game with my schoolchildren that works with cross-laterality:

> Sitting on the floor with knees bent, we touch opposite elbows to knees. I ask them to have the first morning sunbeams (elbows) kiss the mountaintops (knees). The little ones merrily touch right to right and left to left. The fours and early fives notice that I am doing something different, but have no clue what it is. The late fives and sixes proficiently touch right elbow to left knee.

So look for this cross-lateral shape to appear. It tells you your child is moving toward academic readiness.

Now a word about crayons. Do you want a sense delight? Buy Filana organic beeswax crayons www.filana.com. Why beeswax? First of all, the colors are so pure and gorgeous; you will have to see the difference for yourself. Also, in terms of educating the child's senses, beeswax crayons are a feast. They actually still smell like honey! And the felt sensation in the hand is delicious. You'll be surprised by the subtle but powerful difference in types of crayons. It is good to have a nice mix of both stick crayons and block crayons. Stick crayons help a child develop proper pencil-holding skills, and block crayons are the best for shading large areas or mixing colors on the page.

- Perhaps your child is less "representational" and follows a geometric developmental progression:
  - The very young child's strokes of color, tracing movement, can eventually become a central cross-form which quarters the page.
  - This cross is the ancient symbol of the self.
  - Look for the day your child draws an X, it's a red-letter day!
  - This cross-laterality signifies a specific stage of brain development.
- Look online for Filana organic beeswax crayons www.filana.com. You will love them! Buy the block crayons for the very young child, and you can switch to the stick as they move toward grade-school readiness.

**Section Five Intention:**

To know the importance of art, to join your child in art, to arrange an art-space at home, and to envision the place of art in a family festival.

I recommend two grades of crayon paper. You can use a ream of simple copy paper for everyday use, when your child wants to sit down and fill page after page with color. It is also a real pleasure to keep a ream of good-quality drawing paper (see Chapter Notes for ordering information) for special occasions: a get-well card for Grandma, or a love picture for a special little friend. Your child can help you choose which paper he wants today. He may simply like the texture of the good-quality paper, and ask for it often. Collect these drawings and gather them into "books" that he can give as gifts at holidays.

To make a gift book, gather the drawings and, with a hole-punch, make three holes down the left side of the page. Now run richly colored ribbons through the holes. Leave the ribbon a bit loose, so it doesn't cut the paper as the pages are turned. These homemade gifts are real "keepers," and will be pulled out often for viewing! (From *Heaven on Earth*)

*Section Five Intention*: to help parents understand the importance of artistic expression for their child. To help parents feel comfortable with their own artistic endeavors, as they sit beside their young artist. To help parents arrange an art-space for their child at home. To help them envision creating a family festival, with the inclusion of artistic experience.

## Week One Interactive Exploration

*This week we look in depth at preparation, materials and introduction of a children's art space.*

- Prepare an art-space for your child at home. I always feel the kitchen is the best place for art to happen, because cleanup is so easy, and as parents work in the kitchen, the children can be close-by making art.

- If you have space, a small table and chairs is best; this way your child can independently follow their interests and make art as they are called. If not, the dining table is perfectly fine, if you don't mind the creative chaos that may ensue.
- A low kitchen cabinet can be designated for art supplies.
- Supplies you'll want, for "everyday art":
  - A ream of copy paper. Save the art paper for festival preparation or gift-making. Give your child about 10 clean pages to work with; when they are filled with art, give 10 more.
  - A good selection of beeswax crayons. Look for the new all-organic beeswax crayons from Filana.
  - A pair of children's scissors, old *National Geographic* magazines and school glue.
  - As your child becomes five or six: the inner roll of toilet paper, tissue boxes, colored construction paper, cardboard boxes and masking tape. Be amazed at their artistic sculptures.
  - As your child becomes seven or eight, collect bigger cardboard boxes, for constructing "real" houses they can tape together, with cut out doors to adjoin. Don't forget windows, and of course they'll need to paint curtains and door trim and much more. These "art sculptures" can be in construction mode for days and days!
  - Don't forget play-dough (recipe, *Heaven on Earth*, p. 155).
- Introduce the art-space to your child by joining him in coloring a picture. As you finish yours you can say "I'll write the story of my picture" Then at the bottom of the page, write a sentence or two about your picture, or actually make a little story. This is a beginning foundation for literacy: our thoughts can be represented not only by images, but also by symbols—words. Perhaps when he finishes, he'll say "Here is my story." If so, write down his words for him, and read them back. This is powerful magic for a child. This does not want to become a lesson or an early reading program. It is simply the way literate people live their lives, with images and words both spoken and written.

**Week One Exploration**
- Create your child's art-space.
  - The kitchen is my favorite place for art, where is yours?
  - A small table and chairs are helpful, but the dining table works, too.
  - Keep every-day art materials close by:
    - A ream of copy paper, put 10 clean pages out each day
    - Beeswax crayons, Filana are great
    - Children's scissors, old National Geographics or good photo magazines, and school glue
    - For 5s and 6s, try household sculptural materials like empty TP rolls, tissue boxes, construction paper, masking tape.
    - For 7s and 8s, larger cardboard boxes can become houses!
    - Play-dough is great, make it yourself.
- Introduce this space by joining her in making art!

*Write your thoughts and Talk with your partners.*

- Until your child becomes comfortable going to make art on her own, you can join her as she colors, but I imagine it won't be long before she fully inhabits the space and fills your life with art!

*Weekly Pages*

**Vision and assessment:** How does this art-space work for you? How does it fit into your family's rhythm? Art is something that can be done alone...in the company of loved ones. A perfect balance. How comfortable are you in making art? If you are timid, let go of any expectation that you create "form"; just relax and enjoy the colors as they go on the page. Collage is also a wonderful way to loosen up. Join your child in choosing and cutting images, then layering them in intuitive ways on your paper. Relax and enjoy!

**Conversation Notes:** Here's a fun idea: let your conversation about art *be* an artistic adventure. Make art together, and then tell each other the "story"!

## Week Two Interactive Exploration

*This week, let's begin to imagine the role of art and craft in one of your family's yearly festivals, a mid-November Lantern Walk.*

Reread chapter 3 in *Heaven on Earth* to refresh your memory of the fundamentals of festivals, and the section in chapter 7 about watercolor painting. We'll make a paper lantern!

- Two weeks before your chosen date, take out the watercolor paints and good heavy watercolor paper.
- Together, paint with warm red, yellow, gold, and orange. Set these aside to dry. Paint again the following week, or a few days later. You want to have a number of paintings to choose from for lantern making or to have enough to make a lantern for each member of the family.

- Often, when we make art for a festival, we work collaboratively with our child. He has helped by making the luscious colored paintings. Now you can ask him to "help" by watching and giving ideas.
- Choose the finest completely dry paintings. Cut them to be 8 inches by 12 inches. Fold 2 inches from the bottom. Snip at 1-inch intervals from the bottom to the fold. Your paper will now have a fringe on the bottom.
- Place the painting on a pad of newspaper, on the table. With a utility knife begin to cut stars, moons, comets, the sun, falling stars….the night sky appears before your eyes!
- Now, gently bend the paper to make a tube and staple it at the top and above the fold. You will need a heavy-duty stapler with a long arm.
- With a hole-punch, make a hole one-half inch from the top, at the point where the cylinder joins.
- Make another hole directly across; these will be where the handle attaches.
- Your fringe pieces will naturally begin to spiral inward to create the bottom of the cylinder.
- With gold or yellow duct tape, fasten these together to secure your bottom, both outside and inside the cylinder. You can cut a circle from another painting, if you'd like, and glue it on top of the exterior duct tape.
- You can make the handle out of various types of wire; the kind I like I buy at the craft store. It is a medium weight and has raffia wrapped around it.
- You will want the handle to be 12 inches high, so cut a length of wire 14 inches long
- Loop a 1½-inch piece of wire through each hole. Bend the wire up and wrap it around itself to secure the handle.
- With duct tape or glue, attach a votive candle to the bottom of the cylinder.
- With your child, admire your lovely lantern!

**Week Two Exploration**

Make a paper Lantern for an autumn lantern Walk!

- Make several watercolor paintings in autumn colors.
- Follow the directions on this page … voila' a few lovely autumn lanterns!
- On the festival evening, begin the walk just after sunset, before it is truly dark.
- Go singing through your neighborhood.
- Come home to a Harvest Meal!

*Write your thoughts and Talk with your partners.*

On your festival evening, begin your walk just after sunset. Kindle all the little lanterns for your family. You can go walking and singing through your neighborhood, or through the dusky woods, as the crisp fallen leaves rustle at your feet. Remind your child this is a lantern *walk*, not a run. Help them be aware that as the sky darkens their lantern glows more brightly! Return home just as the stars really begin to shine and darkness has fallen. Enjoy a festive harvest soup (see *Heaven on Earth*, p. 55) and a harvest loaf (p. 61) together. Go to bed with images of your little light shining into the darkening world!

## Weekly Pages

**Vision and assessment:** What was your original vision/imagination of this Lantern Festival? How did you imagine the lantern making would enrich the experience for your child? How did the actual experience reflect your planning? Make notes not only on the painting activity—what worked and didn't, what to do differently—but also on the whole experience of art incorporated into your festival life!

**Conversation:** Brainstorm ways to incorporate art into other festivals; make notes, plan ahead and enjoy!

# WEEKLY PAGES

# Section Six

## STORY ESSENTIALS
## THE WONDER OF STORIES

One of our most human capacities is the ability, as well as the inherent need, to create stories. It is through the medium of story that we make meaning of our life. We each have our own personal story, which dynamically changes as our understanding and integration expand. Bruno Bettelheim tells us that the young child achieves "understanding, and with it the ability to cope, not through rational comprehension...but by becoming familiar with (life) through spinning out daydreams—ruminating, rearranging, and fantasizing about suitable story elements in response to...[life] pressures."[10]

Through the use of story, we can give our children the powerful tools needed to make sense of their lives. Stories offer our children examples of solutions for the difficulties they will encounter as they grow and develop. They also image for our children various qualities of character that will aid them in these difficulties. These images can lay a foundation of strength that will serve them for a lifetime. For a "true" story, like all good literature, appeals to readers at many different levels of their being, and also speaks to different stages of development. The stories and potent images we give our children offer new dimensions to their imagination, ones they could find difficult to discover on their own.

Not only does the realm of story help growing children make sense of their inner experience, it can help them understand the way the outer world works, as well. In all early societies, from the most ancient rendering of story as paintings on cave walls through the long and hallowed tradition of oral storytelling, to the evolution of story into print, always story has served the larger society. Through

> • *Stories give your child tools to make sense of life, from offering various qualities of character to imaging positive problem solving. "True" stories speak to many different levels of our being, and stages of development.*
>
> • *They also help the child understand family and societal values, and the human interactions portray qualities both admired and rejected.*

Language acquisition is supported by stories and moves through a developmental progression:

- **For your baby,** simply talk with her as you move from experience to experience: "Is your diaper wet? Let's make you warm and dry" "Here's Daddy, ready to hold his baby" "Let's wash dishes together." She, in her wrap, is rocked by your movements and the sound of water. Remember finger and toe games: they are rhythmic, rhyming and body-based.

- **For two- through four-year-olds,** stories told in verse are best. The rhythm and rhyme of verse calls body memory into play, augmenting verbal memory. And they are pure fun!

- **Stories for three- and four-year-olds** can recreate the experiences of their own days. Nature stories help them understand their own backyard explorations.

- **Five- and six-year-olds** are ready for fairy tales. Life and their own development is giving them challenges. They need images of courage, intelligence, kindness, generosity, and more. Fairy tales offer these through the living language of images.

the images offered, the child is shown the subtleties of human interaction, as well as the qualities both admired and rejected by the social group. In this way stories have shaped social behavior, and culture has been passed on from generation to generation. The fact-oriented nature of history is always embellished with that which captures the human heart, the stories of the people whose lives are involved in the history making.

## Language Acquisition through Story

We cannot underestimate the function of storytelling in the acquisition of language. The child's first impression of the mother tongue occurs in the womb. After birth, the baby is held in his parents' loving embrace, and in the warm flow of language that surrounds him. This is why it is so important to offer the infant and young child the sounds of the natural human voice, and to limit his exposure to mechanical or electronic voices. It is not just the content of the words that is critical to healthy development; it is also the feeling quality, the human quality carried in the voice. The mother holds her baby and talks soothingly during diapering and nursing. "Oh," she says to the baby, "are you wet? Let's make you warm and dry." "You must be hungry!" or "Here comes daddy. He loves his boy!" Already at this early stage, the baby is learning about himself, his world, and those around him through story. In the simple natural verbal recounting of Baby's life, physical sensation, feelings, and eventually images are being created and recreated. Through hearing the "story" of his days unfold, by associating words with people and things, slowly the child begins to live into language.

For the baby, this simple tracking of experience through language can be enriched by "finger and toe" games. The classic rhyme "This little piggy went to market" tells a story in rhyme and gesture. This kind of story is told in Mother or Father's lap, with rhyme and gesture referring to Baby's physical body. It lays a foundation for language development, and also the development of memory, upon which meaningful cognition depends.

Because finger and toe games are rhythmic, rhyming, and bodily based, Baby's verbal memory is augmented by a kind of motor memory in which body sensation calls up the next image or word. The classic nursery rhymes, when repeated again and again with your child in your lap, give the baby, toddler, and preschool child a wealth of experience in rhythmic language and a solid foundation in image formation. This capacity to form mental images is the prerequisite for all academic learning.

You will want a copy of Mother Goose to be one of the first books you buy for your baby. At first, think about using it primarily as a reference book. You can leave it open on the kitchen counter, and as you go about your work, slowly build up your repertoire of the beautiful, funny, and nonsensical rhymes it contains. While holding Baby on your lap, make eye contact, and in the spirit of fun, repeat the rhymes in a slow, clear, rhythmic fashion. Using "This little piggy went to market" as a model, you can punctuate the end-rhymes with a tickle of fingers, toes, nose, ears, belly button, and so on. Be certain that you use the same gestures in the same way each time you say a particular rhyme with her. Again, this helps to develop motor and later cognitive memory function.

It is best, for our two-, three- and four-year-old, to find stories that are told in verse, with simple images that reflect her small world. All children love the rhyme and rhythm of poetry, so check your library and bookstore. Elegant use of language is a treasure in these times when much of modern children's literature has become "cute-ified," with the language reduced to its lowest common denominator. We want to offer our children, beginning at an early age, language that is richly textured, varied, and melodic. If we think of language as a river in which our children are carried along, let us look to the quality, purity, and life force of this water. (Check the bibliography for book ideas.)

## Stories for Three- and Four-Year-Olds

Stories that re-create for our children's activities from their own days—the warm brown smell of oatmeal in the morning, the acrobatics of the squirrel in the tree outside the kitchen window, cool silken sand between bare toes—these stories help them bring language to their everyday life, and thereby make sense of it. In your library, you can search for picture books that tell the story of simple happenings that occur in the course of a simple life. For your very young children, see if you can find the ones with little story line, just poignant illustrations of an event. Simplicity is the watchword here, as it is in most choices you make for your young child. Look for stories that picture, for instance, a young child's experience of a kitten purring in her lap, or the wonder of waking up snuggled in the blankets as a bird sings outside the window.

You may also discover the wonder of "wordless books," which tell a story in pictures only. These are not only delightful for your child, who can relax and gaze wonderingly at the progression of pictures, but also for you! They provide you an opportunity to practice your skill at creating stories. Your child can join you in story making, also, if you point to a picture and say, "I wonder what is happening here." A homemade story is a gift from heart to heart.

Three- and four-year-olds are busy becoming aware of the natural world. They are like little buddhas—very present in the sense impressions that each moment offers. Nature offers them a subtly and slowly changing variety of sensory input within a broad context of constancy. Because they are still very natural beings, they are attracted to the green world outdoors. Books and stories that sensitively render the simple splendors of the interconnected web of life are perfect at this age. You might find in your library an illustrated story of the yearly cycle of a tree, as it buds, flowers, leafs out, drops its leaves, and finally makes nuts or berries, which the deer come to eat. Or perhaps you could find one that creates a picture of a little child wishing for snow as she blows out the evening candle. Then the silent descent of tiny diamonds, till at dawn her house is nestled in snowdrifts. Simple, simple simple.

A perfect way for a three- or four-year-old to understand the interdependent relationships in nature is through the story imagery of a large and loving extended family. We can read and perhaps create our own stories of Mother Earth as she cares for her many "children," the leaves, insects, and small animals. We can describe how she puts them to bed in the fall, keeps them warm in winter with a snow-white blanket, and wakens them to wear their flower dresses in the spring. Other family members are Father Sun, Sister Rain, and Brother Wind, who each play a significant role in the ordering of life on Earth. You can make up stories that tell of the "Weather Fairy Family," the rain fairies who come to care for the spring garden, the mist fairies who sprinkle pearls along the spine of each blade of grass, the snow fairies bringing warm white blankets for winter. Your children are just discovering the nature of "family" firsthand, and will love to hear their own experience portrayed in this imaginative way.

Animal stories are also excellent for three- and four-year-olds. You will want to focus on stories about animals that are familiar to your children, through their backyard experiences, and save the savanna animals of Africa or marsupials of Australia for a later stage of development. Stories of family pets, farm animals, backyard wildlife, insects, and water creatures are good at this age. You will want to look for imaginative renderings of these, a kind of anthropomorphism, rather than a scientific examination. We want our children to develop, at this age, a feeling quality for the animals and for nature. This they can do by beginning to form inner pictures that are born out of their own experience. Remember to put your little one in your lap and read slowly, allowing time for him to "digest" the language as well as the images. Your child will ask for the same story over and over, and it is important that you read the text in the same way each time to strengthen his language acquisition, memory, and sequencing. This "layering up" of visual, auditory, and tactile experience is a gift we can give that will last a lifetime.

After a little practice making up finger and toe games with Baby, and creating stories to go with the wordless books, we will enjoy the next natural step. If we make ourselves familiar with the simple, home-oriented themes appropriate to our three- and four-year-olds, we can begin to really take pleasure in the adventure of making up stories of our own imaginings. Remember to keep the themes close

to home and familiar. Keep the plot very minimal. Allow the clarity
of the images you create to carry the day.

### Fairy Tales for Fives and Sixes

For children of five and older, though, a need for something
new emerges. With their newly found skill levels, with the corollary
independence this brings, and with maturing cognitive development,
children now need images they can turn toward for courage, intelligence, and generosity. This is the time for the introduction of fairy
tales. Fairy tales will serve the needs of the developing child until
seven or eight years of age. Like all true world literature, fairy tales
speak to all ages and stages. We parents, too, can take meaning and
guidance from the tales we choose for our children.

The child of five or six is beginning to experience the presence
of "good and evil" in her own life. She may experience this in being
teased by other children while at the park, or even in the simple
interactions of visiting cousins! Generally the young child is not yet
capable of recognizing these oppositions within her own being, but
she certainly recognizes them in her outer world. Well-chosen fairy
tales can show her, through simple, clear imagery, and characters
that are painted in broad strokes, positive ways to deal with the
condition of her humanity. These tales can help to shape her moral
development, as well.

Fairy tales characteristically state a problem in clear, unmistak-
able terms. The plot is laid out simply, and the characters are drawn
in bold, unambiguous strokes—the evil queen is, truly, evil incar-
nate, the youngest son has a pure and golden heart. It is imperative
for the child of this age that the characters embody qualities rather
than complex human individuals. The child does not yet possess the
discernment necessary to evaluate figures drawn more closely to life,
figures filled with the ambiguities that are true of us all.

At this point, the child needs to see the various "qualities" of
the human soul laid out in understandable terms, personified in the
different figures in the tale. We see opposite qualities laid side by

side: one sister is virtuous and industrious, the other lazy and cunning. One brother is selfishly cruel, the other compassionate. One parent is all good, the other all bad. Laying these opposites side by side gives the child the opportunity to see what these characteristics bring to fruition in the lives of the figures as the story unfolds. The cruel brother is turned to stone, while the compassionate one wins the love of the princess forever. And is it not true that cruelty hardens the heart, while kindness opens the doors of love? The lazy sister is covered in "pitch," while the industrious one is clothed in gold. We know only too well that our inner laziness creates lethargy, while inner striving, regardless of outer result, shines out in wealth of heart. Seeing these opposites laid side by side, the child can begin to imagine what kind of person she would like to become. She does this by identifying with the various characters, feeling what they feel and "trying on" different ways of being. Often in fairy tales the negative figure has temporary ascendancy, and the child may feel attracted to the power, cunning, or might of this figure. As the story unfolds, the child is shown the result of such an egoistic orientation, and can experience this imaginatively.

The young child does not yet possess the conceptual ability to "choose" between right and wrong; rather, she identifies with the character that arouses her sympathy or antipathy. The more simply and clearly the character is drawn, the easier it is for the child to identify. And we must keep in mind that it is not the figure's essential "goodness" that appeals to the child; instead she identifies with the condition of life that this goodness creates. Through these tales, she learns that goodness brings good results into her life, and that egoism eventually brings great limitation into life.

Some fairy tales do not so clearly lay out the opposites; rather, they pose a question and show solutions. The child can see in the diverse figures of the story that there are many different kinds of people, and various ways to approach problems. The little girl outwits the bear and finds her way home. The poor woodcutter generously shares his crust of bread and is given sustenance forever. The youngest brother looks kindly on the bees, which then help him choose the sweetest princess. The prince goes out into the world, and by his own pure heart and perseverance at the tasks given him, he wins the princess and the kingdom as well. The girl must sit vigil three nights and withstand the visitation of monsters to discover that the kingdom is rightfully hers. We adults can all relate to the above fairy-tale themes: A keen intelligence "outwits" the most confounding circumstances. Generosity begets generosity tenfold. Kindness toward others brings much-needed help into our own lives. Purity and perseverance make our hearts rich.

Calmly facing our inner "monsters" returns us to our true selves. What better way for us to pass on to our children these hard-won truths than to give them the actual "felt experience," as they identify with the fairy-tale characters? (from *Heaven on Earth*)

*Section Six Intention*: To help parents understand the critical necessity of *good* stories, in the life of their child: to know that stories have nutritional value for the soul in a similar way that food nourishes the body. Junk food creates malnourished bodies and junk stories create malnourished souls (this is true for adults, too!) To help parents not only choose good stories for their children, but to create their own stories "made by heart"!

## Week One Interactive Exploration

*This week, we write our own lives as a fairy tale.*

- Here is a remarkable way to understand quickly how powerful the role of story is, in the life of a young child: consider your own childhood as a fairy tale. Begin to shape and imagine what the fairy tale of your childhood and young adulthood would be—an adventure story? An animal tale? A princess consigned to scullery work? You, of course, are the hero. Who are the supporting characters? Who are the helpers, and who are the

---

**Week One Exploration**

Want to learn the *power* of Story? Write you own life as a fairy tale! You are the hero. Who are your helpers, who the challengers? Into what unknown lands has the journey taken you? What has brought despair, where is hope found? Find the Gold in your life story!

◦ Make pictures, draw feelings, write haiku, make a collage.

◦ Put this all together: your book will be filled with your soul. Very powerful medicine!

*Write your thoughts and Talk with your partners.*

challengers? Upon what journey have these challenges sent you? What support has come mysteriously and unbidden? What lessons learned...or not learned and needed to be relived? What despair? What hope? What grace? What second chances? What magic? This is a deep invitation to *"Find the Gold"* in your life.

- This story of your life is for your adult consideration; we'll work next week on making stories for your child.
- As parts of your story unfold, through the week, jot down the images, the memories, the feelings.
- Make pictures, draw feelings, create the images of your inner life.
- Write a haiku. Let words shape themselves.
- Begin to sense the story line.
- Gather images from magazines, make a collage.
- Put this all together as a book—your own fairy tale. If you have given yourself to this task, your story will be full of meaning, imbued with your soul.
- *This* is what Story is, to your young child!

**Weekly Pages:** Include your own fairy tale in this workbook. Go back to it from time to time; notice how the story may have changed, or add another chapter.

**Conversation Notes:** You will, no doubt, have lots to talk about with your partners this week! Discuss and make notes of the impact of this "life as fairy tale" exercise. Talk about how this new knowledge will affect your choice of stories for your child.

## Week Two Interactive Exploration

*This week we create a handmade story for our child.*

- The fairy tale of your life was written for your own deepening, not for your children's ears!
- Now we'll explore "When I was a little girl/boy" stories, that you tell especially for your child! In these stories, we have artistic license: when I tell these stories to my class children,

I tend to gloss over the deficiencies of my parents, or I make them comic and charming. I also tell of times I didn't manage to obey and life-lessons learned (although my mom said "carry the pie with two hands" I was sure I could do it with one—and the sorrow of scooping cinnamon apples and flaky crust off the floor, for instance).

- Think of the day you loved most, each week, or the "family play time" you waited for with anticipation.
- Fill your story with sense information: the way the spaghetti sauce made your mouth water, the way the skinned knee didn't hurt until you noticed the blood, how your father bent toward the tomato plant to pick the reddest cherry tomato for you....
- Tell your child a story; see if it leads to more!
- Enjoy the process.

**Weekly Pages**: Write down the stories you are creating. Your children will cherish this memoir, especially when they want to tell stories to *their* children!

**Conversation notes**: This is easy: talk to your partner about the emerging memories; give each other ideas about editing, including images and sense descriptions. This should be fun!

## Week Three Interactive Exploration

*This week we look at the therapeutic power of stories.*

- This week, we'll work with the idea of a "therapeutic story." Go to chapter 6 in *Heaven on Earth* for in-depth discussion of the principles of a therapeutic story.
- What situation in your child's life do you see him struggling with or in conflict about? What life lesson is coming his way? More subtly, what quality of character would benefit her, in a life situation? Is he feeling too shy to join a group of boys in play? Would she benefit from a sense of generosity?

---

**Week Two Exploration**

Now we make a story for our child. How about "When I was a little girl/boy?" Think of ways your childhood parallels theirs: A favorite meal? A game of imagination that went on forever? A goofy mistake you made? The way your dad played with you?

- Use images, not concepts.
- Use detailed sensory descriptions.
- Keep it light and fun.
- Use artistic license.
- Enjoy the process!

*Write your thoughts and Talk with your partners.*

- Shape a story in which the characters (animals or humans) experience the same situation or emotions as your child. Lay out the situation in simple clear terms. Lightly describe the feelings. Perhaps through a magical helper, or through a chance encounter, the main character is given the insight or qualities s/he needs.
- Show through the conclusion how our hero/heroine's life is fuller and happier with this new capacity.
- Tell this story three nights at bedtime. Allow the images to act as leavening yeast.
- Here is one piece of magic: Include a little song, as you tell the story at night. You can hum it to yourself—nearly under your breath—at breakfast or throughout the day. When you observe your child in the situation the story was designed for, stroll through the room with this tune barely audible. Allow your children to "find" the story and its message all on their own... with a little magic from you.

**Weekly Pages**: Again, write down the story you have created, the creation process as well as the experience of telling it. Write your child's response and yours, too. Here is an advanced piece of homework: think of a situation in *your own* life and make a therapeutic story for yourself, or find a fairy tale that can give you the inner images *you* need.

**Conversation notes**: Share this process with your partners. Share how you constructed the story to reflect your child's need. Share the evolving results. Stay tuned for further chapters. Think of other situations that might need a helpful story.

## Week Four Interactive Exploration

*This week we research* **good** *stories.*

- This week is a research week for you. Review the introductory thoughts and chapter 6 *in Heaven on Earth* to understand the

---

**Week Three Exploration**

Now let's think of the healing power of our stories. We'll make a curative story for our child. Reread chapter 6 in *Heaven on Earth*.

- Is there a struggle or a conflict that could use a little help? ... or a quality of character that needs to be nurtured?
- Let your story animals or human beings have a situation similar to that of your child.
- Simple clear images are best.
- Who is the helper, or how is the situation or emotion brought full circle for resolution?
- Tell the story three nights at bedtime; it will act as a "yeast."
- Make note of any subtle changes in your child to the situation.

*Write your thoughts and Talk with your partners.*

**Week Four Exploration**

This is a research week, so get ready to explore and read! Review the Introductory thoughts and also chapter 6 in *Heaven on Earth* for a better understanding of your child's literary developmental needs. Now check out the web-sites on this page, browse around, talk with your partners, rummage on-line, and mostly enjoy this meander through pure beauty.

*This will be a fun week to write your thoughts and Talk with your partners.*

developmental sequence of age specific stories. Begin to gather stories for your child's developmental stage right now, and also stories for the future.

- Look on-line for sources of Waldorf books, such as:
  www.steinerbooks.org
  www.waldorfbooks.org
  www.waldorflibrary.org
  www.thecityschoolla.org/waldorf-childrens-book-list
  www.waldorfpublications.org/collections/children-s-books
- Think about birthday and holiday gift giving; the tradition of a new book for holidays can continue for a lifetime, to nourish your child's soul. Even into young adulthood!

**Weekly Pages:** Keep an on-going list of the good books you'd like to be in your child's life.

**Conversation Notes:** Share these with your partners. Give each other inspiration. Plan to trade books occasionally, too!

# WEEKLY PAGES

## Section Seven

# Let Them Play!

Play is the heart of childhood, the foundation of our humanity. We can retain the ability to be playful as we grow, and a playful, flexible mind is a measure of health and grace, even into old age. Humanity is given a very long period of infancy and childhood. During this extended infancy, the brain is "wired together" for efficient learning and functioning, which will serve us the rest of our life. When we watch our little children play, we are filled with tenderness at their innocent worldview, filled with gods and fairies. However, if we study more closely the brain development that takes place in these years, we will stand in awe, thunderstruck at the marvel of each child.

### *Movement and Play*

We say that children "learn by doing." This is a common way of saying that the learning process is a miraculous orchestration and integration of the entire body, moving a million tiny interconnected particles toward the "gestalt" that is meaning. Children think through movement and play. In movement and play the brain goes through all the complex processes of growth and learning. The main avenue through which the child perceives the world is the realm of the senses. Through the natural sensory input of play, the child actively makes the world his own, rather than remaining a passive observer. Neurophysiologist Carla Hannaford, author of Smart Moves, says, "The richer our sensory environment and the greater our freedom to explore it, the more intricate the patterns for learning, thought, and creativity will be.... Our sensory experiences, both external and internal, shape our way of imaging and

- Play is the heart of childhood! Children think through play. They make their world understandable as they "play though" new experiences. In their sensory-rich and movement-imbued play, they gain mastery. They come to know themselves and their place in the world.
- What do we mean by *Play?*
  - It is self-initiated and self-directed, not coached or taught.
  - Through movements both fine and large, the child interacts bodily and soulfully with the environment and others.
  - It is not scripted by media images.
  - No device stands between the child and the sense world.
  - The "toy" is an empty vessel for the child's imagination; it speaks, walks, moves and interacts only through the child's imagination and physical manipulation.
- We can recognize pure play by the sense of "flow" the child experiences. This is the same neurological state of being an elite athlete or long-time meditator experiences. It is pure joy!

> Movement is essential in childhood! *Play is the Way.*
>
> ◦ Movement weaves all the unique and specific brain structures together for optimal relationship with life.
>
> ◦ Movement integrates an ocean of sensory information; your child makes meaning...makes sense of life...when she can heartily and joyfully Play!

therefore, our thinking."[11] *The life force through which the young child plays will eventually grow into cognitive thought.*

If we watch a young child at play, we can see that through her constant sensory/physical interaction with the environment, she gains experience and understanding of the situation, of herself, and the relationship between the two. She comes to know herself, the world, and what flows between. A baby sees a bright, round object and reaches for it. At some point she manages to push the ball, and now she sees the colors dance. Eventually she learns that, when she moves in such a way, she has the pleasure of the dancing colors.

She learns, through the open exploration of the senses, in other words through play, that she has impact not only on the world, but also on her inner experience. The movement of reaching for the ball, or any purposeful movement, sets in motion a cascade of neural communication that creates a foundation for lifelong learning.

Through this sensory-rich play, the child gains a certain mastery over her body, and her world. She also begins to understand the inner world of emotional experience. It is critical that, through play, the different areas of the brain that control thought and emotion begin to communicate. "The frontal lobe," Hannaford writes, "is able to synthesize thought with emotion through...the limbic system to give us compassion, reverence for life, unconditional love, and all-important play."[12]

When a child's younger sibling is born, she can make this experience her own through play with her doll. She can feed, bathe, and nurture her doll. She may also work through aggressive feelings by "sending brother back" and stuffing the doll into a corner. Day-by-day, she vacillates, experimenting with how feelings work and what she wants to do with them. Usually if there is a very new and potent experience in the life of the young child, you will see it reflected in her play. Given time, given your own quiet observation of the process and your capacity to "hold" your child in love, you will see the experience become integrated. Your child will develop the new and necessary qualities. As neural pathways are forged in the brain, essential qualities grow in the heart.

Children are always in motion, constantly "doing." Movement activates the brain's neural wiring, making the whole body the instrument of learning. It is our task, as parents and educators, to allow children this necessary motion in an environment that encourages purposeful movement. Especially in these times of ever-increasing overstimulation of the senses through the media, through technology, and through our hectic pace of life, we must create play environments that allow the child to discover the world at his own pace through purposeful movement and creative imagination. We must allow him the freedom to move his body and his world in a way that suits these creative impulses.

But what is purposeful movement for a child? When the child takes in sensory input, a motor response is catalyzed. He sees the ball and reaches for it. He holds the doll and feeds it, or he pushes it away, depending on the purpose of the moment. When children are deprived of movement, either by the physical immobility created by media exposure or by early academic programs that keep them still, sitting in a chair, the imperative to move becomes constricted. Then, when movement is finally allowed, it is as though a dam breaks, and the movement can become hyperactive or erratic. Another response to constricted movement can be a fear of movement, or a flaccid approach to movement.

## Play educates head, heart, and hands

The astonishing width of a child's imagination reminds me of the grand excesses of the natural world. Our children are Nature's crown jewel, giving a human voice to Her great imagination of what this earth might become. Can we sacrifice tidiness during playtime in order to allow our children the capacity to move their bodies and their world (our living room) toward a deeper understanding of life?

It is critical that we allow our children the full progression of the development of play. The entire process builds a firm, resilient foundation for all of their academic work. The culmination of play, or the ability to create and hold inner images, is the fundamental

prerequisite for all academic learning. In fact, it is this very force of the creative imagination that naturally evolves in time into the capacity for conceptual thought.

As we not only allow our children to move purposefully in their play, but also create play environments that foster this broad, diverse creative imagination, in the same measure we strengthen their future capacity for our most fundamental human activity, thinking. When we give our children a very physical and sensory-based education in play, and allow them to play through many realms of human experience, we offer them a great gift. We offer the possibility that *their future life of thought will be imbued with feeling, and with the ability to bring this heartfelt thought into action in the world.* This integration of heart forces, thinking capacity, and the ability to act with confidence is essential as we move together into our new century and create the world anew, day by day.

## Outdoor Play

I have found in my many years of teaching young children, and in my years as a mother of young boys, that most children are happiest at play outdoors. Young children are close to the realm of nature because they are still very natural beings.

Because their consciousness is not yet separated from the environment, because they still live in the consciousness of oneness, of unity, they belong still to the natural world. In time they will belong to themselves, as the process of individuation becomes complete. But for about the first seven years, they are still at one with the world they inhabit. The process of separating from the parents and from the environment buds only around age seven. Before that, the child is moved along by life, something like the way a tree's leaves dance in the breeze. The young child responds to the environment in a very unself-conscious way, a very natural way, and the open, complex, and diverse environment of the outdoors gives him that opportunity. If, in his excitement at a butterfly, he needs to dance and pirouette dizzyingly around the garden, no one has to

- Play transforms into thought.
  - When allowed time to play, the same exuberant joyful curiosity can generate your future adolescent and young-adult thinking.
- **Creativity** is the watchword for 21st-century education. We foster this essential creativity-for-the-future right now, as we create engaging play spaces.

say, "Be careful of the table." If he needs to shout for glee or weep for sorrow, he is free.

If we are fortunate enough to have woods or a natural meadow we can visit often, or that adjoins our yard, our child will have an even more diverse experience of the natural world. Children become connected to the web of life by seeing the relationships between plants, insects, wildlife, and human beings. This "thinking from the whole" is what our children will incorporate into their own being. Our own backyard can be the foundation of environmental education and a journey of discovery for the whole family.

## Play and Movement Ideas for Indoors and Outdoors

Play is crucial to children's cognitive development. It is through play that the child takes sense experience and organizes it into complex mental and emotional patterns.[13]

A three-year-old will play "making dinner" at a toy stove. You may be offered the same bowl of soup over and over again. Here we see the development of motor skills, eye–hand coordination, and the budding of care and nurturance, to mention only a few abilities. The five-year-old's game becomes more elaborate. She and her sister may have spent the last hour in the "hospital" bandaging all the stuffed animals' wounds with baby powder and toilet paper, and now, acting as not only the vet but also the restaurant owner, she stands at the toy stove making pizza for all her patients. Having built the pizza delivery truck of chairs and pillows, Sister is ready, and off she zooms.

The learning that takes place in a well-developed imaginative scenario like this is astonishing. Eye–hand coordination, both large and small motor skills, balance, movement, motor planning, social cooperation, emotional self-monitoring, speech, hearing and language development, as well as the remarkably elastic conceptual skills of imagination and thought, are all employed in the world of make-believe. See the chapter on Indoor Play to learn more about the necessity for play in childhood, as well as how to create optimal

**Take them outdoors!**
- Humanity evolved outdoors; we belong there.
- Nature offers the widest sense and movement opportunities.
- Nature exists in a unitive state and so does your young child.
- In an ant carrying a seed to her babies, your child sees a hologram of the web of life.
- She knows innately that she also belongs to this vast family of living beings.

**Section Seven Intention**

To help parents rethink and recreate indoor play space. To inspire a handmade toy. To reimagine the backyard play space. To reinvigorate the family nature connection.

play spaces. Much of modern preschool children's time is now taken up by either structured activities, such as "enrichment classes," or passive activities like media exposure. The prime imperative for the young child is movement through play. It is our responsibility to make as much time available for imagination-rich play as possible.

You will want to choose, from the many ideas offered in this book, where you would like to begin to enrich your child's movement and play environments. Choose just one idea, implement it, experience the magic, incorporate it into your family life, and then choose the next! (from *Heaven on Earth*).

*Go to pages 17 and 18 in* Heaven on Earth *for a delightful list of vigorous outdoor and indoor play activities that will nourish your child's body, heart, soul, and spirit!*

**Section Seven Intention:** To help parents re-think and rearrange the indoor play space, weed out toys and re-organize the remaining ones. To inspire parents to create a handmade toy for their child. To rethink, reorganize, and enrich the backyard play space. To understand the foundational necessity of the nature connection for the child and the family.

## *Week One Interactive Exploration*

*This week we work with the indoor play space.*

- Begin by assessing the indoor play space or spaces. Remember that your young children want and need to be close to you. If the play room is at a distance, reimagine how the toys and playthings can be incorporated into the "common rooms" of the house, the kitchen, dining, and living room. If your house has a great room, with all these common rooms combined, you are in luck. If not think about this:

◇ Which toys belong in the kitchen? Think of indoor sandbox, art table, and children's kitchen equipment.

◇ Which belong in the dining room? How about fort building materials: sheets, clothespins, finger-knit ropes, some throw pillows, small cotton rugs. And a hardwood floor is a great place for block-play, because the block cities remain more stable than when built on a rug. And...what else?

◇ Which toys go in the living room? You might like a toy house, furniture, and a family of small dolls; wooden castles and knights; and baby dolls, cradles, a basket of silks, dress-ups, hats, and crowns.

- Now assess the actual toys: remember *Less is More!* The toys mentioned above are the basics. Beyond that you can sort through and decide which toys can be stored in a closet and be brought out at a later season, and which toys simply need to be given away. Rotating toys seasonally is a good idea if you have too many. Nevertheless, the best idea is to weed out the toys that do not foster a wide, free creativity.

- Be sure each play space has low shelves for storage. Various sized baskets are perfect for organizing, and your child's brain development will be enhanced! No more jumbled chaos of the toy chest!

- Now rearrange toys, furniture, shelves in the way you have imagined. Stay attuned to your child's needs and make small changes as necessary.

- This process may take more than one week; be gentle with yourself, and be sure you enjoy it yourself!

**Weekly Pages:** Remember this is an on-going process, as you fine-tune both the arrangement of the play spaces as well as the toys. Keep notes as you go along: what works sort-of and what works better.

**Conversation Notes:** Stay in touch with your partners, talk through how the changes impact not just your child's play, but also your

---

**Week One Exploration**

Re-create your indoor play space:

◇ Your children want to be close to you; bring their toys into the kitchen, dining room, or living room. When their play equipment is in the middle of your space, you'll be more mindful of its beauty; less plastic and more wooden toys!

◇ *Less is More* in terms of toys (and nearly everything else, right?) weed out, give away, and rotate seasonally. Which toys to give away? Look above at the definition of *Play* and you'll have a good idea.

◇ You'll want low shelves and sturdy baskets for organizing toys. Sorting is great for your child's brain development, and the chaos of the toy chest will be gone.

◇ This process might take more than a week; be kind to yourself and pat yourself on the back as you build a beautiful play space!

*Write your thoughts and Talk with your partners.*

adult lives. This re-imagining can actually make your life easier and more joyful!

## Week Two Interactive Exploration

*This week we create a hand-made doll!*

- This week will be fun, and your child will be enchanted. Look in the Appendix of *Heaven* for the pattern to **make a "gingerbread doll"**! This pattern is a simple beginning; it is easy, and a lovely little doll can be created in just two or three hours. After the delight and ease of making your first doll, you will probably want to make a whole family of these little friends. You can alter the pattern for different sizes, and alter the clothing for different characters.
- In the Appendix you will find resources for buying all your doll-making needs.
- When choosing colors, remember that the ones close to each other on the color wheel will be most pleasing to the eye. This is true also for the embroidery floss you choose to stitch with.
- After making one or several dolls, choose a basket with a handle that can be *home*. Line it with a soft silk, or a warm flannel square. At cleanup time each day, the little family can be put to bed in their cozy home.

**Weekly Pages:** This will hopefully be a fun week to journal! The best part of making toys for your children is this: what your child sees is the process of love being made visible. Your adult eye might see that the stitches are uneven, but your child sees a steady stream of love.

**Conversation Notes:** Again, have fun with this conversation! You can laugh together at the critical mind that wants to critique the workmanship, that doesn't see the shining face of love.

**Week Two Exploration**

Let's make a doll together!

○ Look in the appendix of *Heaven on Earth* for the "gingerbread doll" pattern.

○ You'll find all your supply needs there too.

○ Keep the colors "simple and undifferentiated," which means close together on the color wheel. Same for the embroidery floss.

○ Make one doll and celebrate!

○ Make a few and give the little family a home in a soft cloth-lined basket.

○ Your child will be enchanted!

*Write your thoughts and Talk with your partners.*

*No self-criticism allowed.*

## Week Three Interactive Exploration

*This week we re-imagine and rework the outdoor play space.*

- If it is winter, you may want to hold this week's plan for spring-time; if not roll up your sleeves, put on your shoes, and head out doors.

- Again, assess: look around your backyard. Following the guide-lines in chapter 5, "Outdoor Play," see which areas are in good shape and which ones need to be re-imagined.

- Think first of the natural features of your yard: plant tall orna-mental grasses and or flowering bushes in the corners: great hiding places and fort-building foundations. Import good sticks and large stones and various sizes, lengths, and weights of logs, bricks, and board ends, to enhance fort building. Seashells, mosses, and bark are also perfect fairy-house building materials.

- Remember to bring straw bales for building and bagged leaves from neighborhood yard raking. Be sure to have some child-sized rakes.

- Sand and water are inseparable, so be sure you have a source for water and sand play. A tub of water, bowls and spoons of varying sizes, and a small indestructible table close to the sand-box is grand. This little table will become a bakery, a cookie factory…and even a jet plane serving food to the passengers!

- Don't forget the swings! Traditional are lovely, but a tire swing is best for spinning games (excellent brain development, too). In addition, a hammock can be both a cradle and a ship on the high seas.

**Weekly Pages:** Sketch out your placement ideas, make lists of mate-rials, write your favorite outdoor play spaces when you were little; imagine, dream, and get to work!

**Conversation Notes:** Creating an outdoor play space is an involved task, so you will have material for conversation for weeks to come; keep notes, so you don't lose any good ideas.

---

**Week Three Exploration**

Now we head outdoors.

- Refer to chapter 5 in **Heaven on Earth** and assess your outdoor play space.

- Re-imagine it with tall, ornamental grasses or flowering bushes for hide and seek games and fort building.

- Import building materials: good sticks, big stones, logs, bricks, board-ends. Bring seashells home from the beach, and pine cones from a walk in the woods.

- Haul bales of straw and bags of autumn leaves. Small rakes, too.

- A sandbox is essential and water play is its best companion.

- Swinging is great for brain development, so plan for a swing and maybe a hammock, too!

*Write your thoughts and Talk with your partners.*

## Week Four Exploration

*Let's look at the Nature Connection.* How do we model love for the natural world? Bring our daily life outdoors!

◦ The table can be the heart of your outdoor life. Choose a sturdy, not-too-beautiful table. We want the children to make art, build forts under and around, make ramps and other artifact of magic right here at the table. Try a second-hand store.

◦ How about putting the table right in the midst of the play-space, not on a deck or patio? It is more available for games if it is easily accessible.

◦ Bring meals outdoors. Think of sweaters for chilly weather and fans for the heat.

◦ Try art-in-the-park: crayon, play dough, paint, craft. All under the umbrella of the trees.

◦ How about outdoor naps in a little tent? And backyard camp-outs.

◦ Think about a garden: from container gardening on a sunny patio to a full-fledged vegetable patch. Gardening with your child is the best!

*Write your thoughts and Talk with your partners.*

## Week Four Interactive Exploration

*This week we'll explore the Nature Connection, or how we adults model love for and connection to the natural world.*

• Let's look at ways we can bring our daily life outdoors!

• Do you have an outdoor table? This is the place to begin; in the same way that the table is the heart of the home, it can also be the heart and "hearth" of your young child's outdoor experience. So, begin looking for a great picnic table. I would look in second-hand stores: we want to be sure that we don't buy a gorgeous table that we'll worry about, as the children play, make art, build forts around and under, or build ramps upon for the logs to roll down.

• My favorite place for the table is in the midst of the play space, not on a deck. The deck is still part of the "built" environment. If the table is in the middle of the play space, it can become an integral part of many games and activities.

• Think of bringing as many meals outdoors as possible. In chilly weather, put on sweaters and in hot weather run an extension cord to power a windy fan.

• Imagine bringing artistic activities outside: art in the park! Crayoning, playdough, watercolor painting, and crafting can all be done outdoors.

• What about napping outdoors, under a tree, in a little tent?

• Of course, "campouts" in the back yard are the first step toward a lifetime of living in and loving the world of Nature.

• Don't forget about a garden: anything from patio herb and greens planters to a full vegetable plot can spark a child's life-long love for the green outdoors.

**Weekly Pages:** Bringing life outdoors is a lifetime of work. Where did you begin, this week? Did you have a few meals outdoors, or do a little art under the green umbrella of the trees? What have you imagined and begun to plan for the future? Are you thinking of planting some seeds?

**Conversation Notes:** Talk through your ideas/dreams/plans with your partners. Look realistically at what is possible now, at this season. Mark your calendars with good ideas for the future.

## Section 8

# DISCIPLINE AS IMITATION
## THE HEART OF THE MATTER

In Waldorf Early Childhood training we are told that our most important task is to "be a person worthy of the young child's imitation." What exactly is imitation and why is it so important? Cultures worldwide have known the critical function of imitation in nurturing children who will grow to be not only contributors, but gifts, to their society.

Now science can begin to help us understand how this magic works. The scientific term for imitation is *entrainment*. We are born with the astonishing gift of mirror neurons: our brains are designed so that we mirror one another's brain activity; we *entrain* to each other. If I fold the laundry with joy as my young child plays at my feet, his brain will actually produce the same wave patterns and chemical activity as mine do. Whatever I do with my child close by, they will live the same experience through the miracle of mirror neurons. Most important, perhaps, *whoever I am being in the presence of my children is who they are becoming.*

Often when I talk to parents about the profundity of the role of imitation, I see a small wave of panic run through them. "How on earth can we measure up, and show them what it is to be human? We're just regular people." It will be a long time before your children recognize that you are "just regular." The only way I ever learned to carry the weight of my children's admiration, their need and expectation, was to know deep in my bones that I would never ever be perfect or even close. Nevertheless, I also know that Love is perfect—and perfectly reliable. Thus, with all the imperfections that occur in a day, I always relied on Love, knowing in the end all

It is hard for us to comprehend the depth at which our children imitate us. They don't simply imitate what we do, they truly imitate who we are. Whoever I am being in the presence of my child is who he is becoming. The miracle of mirror neurons, the power of my "field of resonance" and his inborn capacity for deep imitation guarantees this dance of becoming.

◊ How do we ever measure up to this task, given all our human limitations and imperfections? Although we are not perfect, Love is! We can rely on our unbounded love for our children to forgive our humanness, our impatience, our hurrying.

◊ We can also verbalize our small transgressions: "I am sorry, I realize now that I hurried you past the box turtle you wanted to see."

◊ And we can practice Heartfulness Meditation.

my transgressions (against my own ideal, by the way, not theirs!) were washed clean by Love's great generosity. So you can relax and enjoy the rest of our discussion about imitation. This time we will examine the process not from a biological standpoint, but from that of "felt experience."

I often think of the young child's capacity for imitation as nutritional. The way the child imitates is akin to the way she digests the food we offer. She simply takes it in, and depending on the nutritional value of the meal, she is well fed or undernourished. By creating indoor and outdoor environments that nourish your child's lifelong learning, and by establishing healthy life rhythms that will nourish your child's sleep times, mealtimes, work and play times, and so forth, you will lay essential foundations for learning.

We can also use this understanding of imitation in the way we approach daily activities. A simple rule is this: if we want the child to do something, then we must do it ourselves, in order to offer him someone to imitate. If you say, "Come brush your teeth," have your toothbrush in hand, too. Or, if it's time for breakfast, be sure you, also, are having a portion. If you wish your child were more active outdoors, put on your jacket, get out the rake and get going yourself.

The young child does not watch us carefully, and then in a studied way choose to imitate, for instance, the tone of our voice as we talk to the cat. Rather, the young child, who is so new to life, simply lives into our actions and makes them her own. We, her parents, are the template of what it is to be human. In the same way that the mother's face is the template upon which all visual learning is based, we are the pattern for what it is to be human. The young child has not yet developed the capacity to recognize her separateness yet. She experiences herself as merged with the environment, and when we understand this, we can consciously arrange ourselves as the emotional environment, and our home as the physical environment, in such a way that she is imitating the best we have to offer.

In each of the many small tasks we do with our child, remember that we are showing him not "our" way, or the regional way. From his perspective, we are offering the secrets of the universe, showing him The Way. So, let's do each thing with as much consciousness as we can bring to the task. Think of the ancient Zen master who rakes the sand garden or pours tea with simple economy of movement and grace.

## Hurrying and Imitation

What about hurrying? This is the disease of our time, and we are all exposed to it in varying degrees. We must each find our own way to inoculate ourselves against it. For if we hurry our family's lives along, our young child will incorporate this hurrying into his own body. Hurrying causes stress, and the American Medical Association tells us that over ninety percent of illness is stress-related.

So practice breathing slowly, observing yourself as you model a task for your child, make mental notes, and try to bring more awareness to it the next time. Because your child imitates everything, she will imitate your comfort, ease, and joy in movement. She will also imitate your deep intention to do it better next time!

But *how* do we, as mere mortals, possibly achieve such a calm, unhurried, expansive, generous attitude toward not just our child, but also Life itself? How do we become that Zen master pouring a cup of tea with economy of movement and grace? How do we embody such Presence?

Just as Zen masters do: we practice! They have the luxury of practicing with eyes lowered in a quiet place. But we need to practice this with our eyes wide open, in motion, and in relationship. A much harder task, but we know a way—Heartfulness Living!

## *Awareness of Family Culture and Self-Discipline Offer Parents a Mirror*

*If we are not satisfied with their behavior, first we must look at the family culture,* or at these areas of our life together: Family Rhythms, Family Work and Play, Child's Play, and the Child's Artistic Expression. We can assess bedtime, nap time and mealtimes. Look also at your

> • Imitation is nutritional: like the way she digests a meal, she simply takes in the environments and experiences we offer. Depending upon their quality, she is well-fed or undernourished.
>
> ◦ For the young child, we parents are her primary environment and experience! We also choose and determine her secondary environments and experiences.
>
> • We are the template of what it is to be human. Let us bring to parenting as much consciousness as we are capable.
>
> ◦ Try breathing slowly; feel peace and joy washing through you, and now bend toward the task of the moment.
>
> ◦ Now do it again. And again...
>
> ◦ Moment by moment. This is spiritual practice.

- When our children misbehave, they offer us a mirror in which to see ourselves.

- If we don't like their behavior, there are steps we can take, beginning with our own self-discipline.

  ◦ First, we look at family culture: has our rhythm changed? Look at bedtime, mealtimes, nap times. Don't forget about downtime. How about work and play? Too many structured activities, too little creative play? What about stories or media influence?

  ◦ Second, we look at our inner rhythm. Are we giving ourselves enough self-care? Enough sleep, healthy food, exercise? Do we need to simplify our time and space? Less computer time, less phone and screen time, less clutter, less stuff.

  ◦ Heartfulness or any meditation is an excellent way to care for ourselves.

child's playtime. Too much structured activity and busyness, or not enough outdoor play? Look at the balance of work and play. Also think about the stories your child has heard, or any media influence. Usually we can see where we have fallen short, and if we continue to observe, we can see patterns emerge, showing specific areas where we need to be particularly attentive. One child might be especially sensitive to the type or the timing of food. Another may need a very firm nap-time; another may need some solitude every day. When we do not give the special attention to specific areas of family life that each of our children needs, they will usually remind us very clearly.

One area that always needs special attention, especially as our society continues to speed up, is family *"downtime."* Families need times simply to be together without an agenda. You can think of it as couch and rug time. In the same way that couples need to find times throughout the days and weeks simply to sit on the couch together, families need these downtimes, too. Perhaps Saturday evenings after dinner and before bath, everyone flops on the couch or rug together. This can be time to play a board game or talk, or roll around on the rug a little bit. Children love for their parents to do a little yoga and stretching on the rug, while they tumble and imitate. This can be a time for everyone to unwind together, and to enjoy simply *being together without doing.* As we weave together the many brightly colored threads of family life, remember to include this quiet neutral shade of happiness.

Second, we must look at our own inner rhythm. The outer rhythm, or structure, needs the support of our strong inner rhythm. Who we are is more critical to our child than what we do, and the very best gift we can give our young child is a happy, well-rested, contented parent. The question each parent must keep alive as we raise our children is, "How do I care well for myself, so that I can care well for them?" Adults, too, need good solid sleep, nourishing food, enough exercise, and a sense of purpose in life. Each parent has to find her own way, and create rhythms for herself, just as we create them for our children. This is not a luxury; it is a "job requirement." We know our children imitate not only everything we do, but also the very way we are human beings. They imitate us from the most concrete activities to the subtlest essence of our being. This can be a paralyzing thought! If, however, we approach ourselves with the same humor and compassion we offer our children, we will be able to appreciate our successes in finding balance, and take our failures in stride as we learn from them.

Balance and rhythm become more difficult as we proceed further into the technological era. It is exactly this difficulty that asks us to continue to work consciously to find balance and inner harmony. How do we accomplish this? A golden rule toward finding this sense of inner rhythm is SIMPLIFY! We can simplify many areas of our lives: the toy shelf, the furniture, clothing, kitchen utensils. The less "stuff" we have to deal with, the more time we have to be at ease.

Third, we find another doorway to balance our inner rhythm is to participate in some activity that truly nourishes us. It is easy for parents to say, "But caring for my family and enjoying the happiness this brings is nourishing for me." This may be true, but before you had children, there were activities that you loved, that nourished you. Find a way to keep them in your life. Or discover new ways to give yourself the satisfaction this brings. Your children need a role model who knows how to find joyful connection with himself and the world. Whether you love to play the guitar or attend the opera, whether you love to bicycle, or bird watch, give yourself these moments. Eventually, sharing what you love with your children will show them how to keep this place of childlike delight open in their own hearts as they mature through life. And your enthusiasm will spill over into all the daily tasks you do with and for them.

Making these inner and outer adjustments—refining our family's rhythms and our child's experience of play and art, and refining our own inner rhythm—this is a lifetime's work! It is not as though we will ever say, "Ah! Now it is all perfect." We will continue to hone these points, on a daily basis, for many years (from *Heaven on Earth*).

---

When you find yourself in the "disciplinary moment," try this process:

- Breathe through your heart and lean toward your child, make eye contact, touch her, bring her into your peaceful space.

- Listen to her: what happened, what does she need?

- Be the Sun.

- Say "Hmmm...I see. Hmmm...let me think about that."

- Stay with simple, non-emotional statements.

- Mirror back what you heard her say.

- Kindly reaffirm what is necessary.

- Say "yes" as often as you can. Tell her when and where she can have what she is telling you she needs.

*What do we do when all aspects are in a good balance, and the children still misbehave?*

Is there a time of day, or a particular situation in which you and your child often come to an impasse? Is there a moment that occurs again and again, and upon reflection, you know you could have responded better, but are not sure how? The following outlines what we have said, above. See if your conscious attention shifts the dynamic:

- Before bed or first thing in the morning, give thought to what aspects in your family's outer rhythm might be contributing to the impasse. Is your child sleep-deprived? Is there too much busyness during the day? Too much car time, not enough play outdoors? Screen time creates many discipline problems, but because screens are omnipresent societally, parents aren't aware of the disturbing influence. Does the family have enough "downtime" together? All of these can contribute to your child being out-of-sorts and uncooperative.

- Now, as you find yourself in the "disciplinary moment," check your inner rhythm: Are you well slept? Have you made time to take care of yourself? Do you have too much on your inner agenda—too many busy thoughts? Make a mental note to balance this. But for now allow your consciousness to rest in your heart and feel the breath moving and rocking you....ahhh....

- Bring your child into your now-peaceful rhythm: make eye contact, put your arm around him.

- See if distraction can work: ask your child to join you in a small task. If there is resistance, and distraction does not work, remember as you move further into the disciplinary moment, to attend to the following:

  **Be the Sun**: *firm and kind* are the watchwords for disciplinary moments. Like the sun, move slowly through the difficult situation. Listen to your child and reply with "Hmmmm, I will think about that." "Oh, I see...let me think." This buys you more time to take a few breaths, and feel its goodness gently blowing through your heart, to settle yourself into this goodness, to feel your own internal rhythms coming into balance. Then make simple, nonemotional statements. "Yes, you'd like to keep running outdoors. It is hard to come in for nap right now. As soon as you wake up, we'll come right back out" In this small conversation you have:

   ◊   quieted yourself
   ◊   listened to your child
   ◊   mirrored back his feeling/wish
   ◊   then stated what needs to happen now
   ◊   found a way to say "yes" to your child's need/desire: "We'll come back outside after nap."

We need to learn to say "yes" to our children as often as possible, so that when we must say "no" it carries weight. Instead of reflexively saying "no," think about saying "yes, this afternoon," or "yes, tomorrow morning," or "yes, when you are older" or "yes, when it is your turn" or "yes, that is a good game to play outdoors, but not indoors," "yes, while you are in the tub," or "yes, it's fine if you're upstairs." Whenever possible, say "yes." You can do this by placing it in the *correct time or place*. New research shows that the human brain does not like to hear the word *no*. It sends cascades of stress hormones showering through the body. For the very young child, let's say "yes" as often as we can—at the right time and in the right place.

Nevertheless, I also feel that, as our children mature, it is essential that they learn to cope with the mild stressors associated with *no*, as well. In the big world there will be plenty of opportunity to hear the word *no*. It is best they hear it first from those who love them most, and who can help them learn to find self-comfort in the face of *no*. Let's "yes" as often as we can, and as our children mature, say "no" often enough to help them develop the resiliency needed to navigate and adjust to its inevitability.

This well-considered process may not stem a torrent of tears. However, you will have moved slowly enough to remember to breathe through your heart to take care of them in the best way. You have modeled for your child how a calm parent navigates the choppy waters of childhood emotions. This shows them how to navigate their own inner turbulence when they grow older.

## *Helping Siblings Negotiate*

Reread pages 202 to 206 in *Heaven on Earth* about children's quarrels and hitting. Even if we have assessed our outer and inner rhythms, have brought the child into our peaceful heart space, have tried distraction, have been firm and kind, have found a way to say "yes" at the right time and place, and have upheld the boundary, we will still have to face sibling quarrels.

You can try this step-by-step process laid out in *Heaven on Earth*:

- Listen to both parties.
- Lay out the problem so they can see how it arose and how their behavior brought about a negative result.
- Show them a positive alternative—a way they can continue to play happily together.
- Don't forget to offer new and interesting ideas as possible paths around a thorny spot.
- If there is still difficulty, now is the time to consider a consequence. Again, check your own heart breathing, take a few breaths….ahhhh…and then speak slowly. Make the consequence logical. Be sure the consequence is related to the improper behavior. Something like this: "Oh, I see. It is still hard for you two to play cooperatively. Now you can have a little time to play alone. We'll try being together again, after a while."

For the five- or six-year-old, after the consequence there might be an occasion to allow the child to "make the world whole again," to rectify the poor behavior and bring harmony. This might come in the form of a beautiful picture drawn for his sister, or a special way he helps you later in the day. If she made marks on the wall, she can help scrub them off and such.

---

**What about sibling negotiations?**

- Listen to both parties.
- Lay out the problem so they can see both sides.
- Show them a positive alternative to their impasse.
- Remember, a new play idea can help them move forward: maybe their pretend family can have two babies, not just one. Like that.
- If a consequence is necessary (often it is not; often help getting past the stuck place is enough) make sure it is logical. If she poured sand on the dog, she can help bathe him.

## Transition Times Need Attention

Our children follow a developmental sequence from birth until they walk into the world as young adults. During times of transition, they stand with one foot in each world as they step out of a particular developmental phase and into another. These times are fraught with uncertainty for the child. One day she may feel all grown up and the next day she may need to curl up in the nest of your family. Or she may need both at the very same time!

These are times when we will be grateful for the hard work we've done to establish and live within the tides of our family rhythms, for these very familiar rhythms will carry you and your child through the rough seas. During these turbulent transition times, we need to assess the many details of our Family Culture and if needed make *minor* adjustments. Transition times are not a good time to do a major overhaul, but slight adjustments can sometimes meet your growing child's needs in a more fine-tuned way.

**Section Eight Intention:** To bring awareness to not only the "disciplinary moment," but also to aspects that support the whole family as they navigate these turbulent waters. Include family downtime, parental self-care, and deepening the Hearfulness way of living.

## Week One Interactive Exploration

*This week we focus on the disciplinary moment.*

Each time your child misbehaves, remember this well-worn path toward successful resolutions. As you practice, it will become habit, a very good habit!

- Check your inner rhythm: breathe and bring yourself into better balance.
- Bring your child into this peaceful heart space; distract with a collaborative task.
- If you need to go further to find resolution, *Be The Sun.*
- Listen; what is your child's need/wish?

---

**Section Eight Intention**

To focus on the disciplinary moment as well as structures that support us while navigating turbulent waters: family downtime, parental self-care, and a deepening Heartfulness way of living.

**Week One Exploration**

- The disciplinary moment. Follow the process outlined on the previous page: Check your heart, bring him close, be the sun, listen, mirror, reaffirm, say when and where "yes" can happen.

- Children's quarrels. Try the next process: Listen, lay the problem out, help with a good idea, follow with a logical consequence (only if necessary).

*Write your thoughts and Talk with your partners.*

- Mirror this back to them.
- Kindly reaffirm what is necessary.
- Say "yes"; place it well within time and space. Say when and where they can fulfill this wish/need.

When negotiating children's quarrels:

- Listen to both parties.
- Lay out the problem and help them see how their behavior created it.
- Show them a positive alternative, so they can get on with the joy of play.
- Offer new ideas for getting past the hard spot.

**Weekly Pages:** Keep notes about what worked and didn't work. Think of ways you could improve. *Is it all too much to keep in mind, in the disciplinary moment?* Just stay in your heart, move and speak slowly and remember the reason is love.

**Conversation Notes:** This is a great week to have a partner! Talk it all through, decide what you'd like to keep and use, re-work the parts that just don't seem right. Listen to your heart. Innovate!

## Week Two Interactive Exploration

*This week will be so much fun! We'll do nothing together.*

Yes, part of discipline is being sure to have downtime as a family. The tensions of the day, which can result in rough spots, can be softened sometimes by *doing nothing* together.

- Think about the best time and space for couch or rug time. Now do it!
- You will be amazed by how thrilled our children are for us to be down on their level, so stretch and roll on the floor. Say "ahhh…" and "ooohhhh…." Let your voice reflect the sweetness of release.

- Yoga is great self-care, so do a little. Nothing serious or silent, just good stretches.
- Sit on the floor, back against the couch, and knit or sew. Chat, laugh, make funny faces, or say poems or nursery rhymes.
- What other ideas?
- Enjoy!

**Weekly Pages:** Be sure to make notes of what was the most fun; sometime when you feel crabby and the thought of downtime is distasteful, reread and be inspired.

**Conversation Notes:** What did your partners think of, that you hadn't? How did everyone like doing-nothing together? Who knew simply being with each other in such a simple way could be so nourishing?

## Week Three Interactive Exploration

*This week, we commit to self-care.*

A well-nourished, well-slept, and happily engaged parent is the prime ingredient for disciplining with love. Let's see how we can help them by helping ourselves. There are many, many suggestions; choose just one and go from there.

- *Physical Self-care:* Pay attention to your own sleep, food, exercise, and work rhythms. What can you tweak to create more balance? Try making small changes over time, not huge shifts all at once. This week, begin with one incremental shift toward nurturing yourself: see the result this brings. Build on this success, and go on to another!
- *Social and Emotional Self-care:* In our society, caring for babies and very young children can be very isolating. Research shows that caregiving rates right up there in the ranks of financial uncertainty or losing a loved one, in terms of creating stress. Human beings are not designed for isolation, especially mothers and babies! Try these ideas:

---

**Week Three Exploration**
*How about self-care?*

- *Physical care:* Think through your sleep, food, exercise, and work time. Tweak things a little for balance.

- *Social and Emotional care:* Stay in touch with friends and their children.

  ◦ Invite a friend and baby for tea; make it a regular date.

  ◦ Join a "Moms and Tots" group; check your Waldorf School.

  ◦ Picnic with another family.

  ◦ Talk with fellow parents; share joys and challenges.

  ◦ Get professional help if you are overwhelmed.

- *Intellectual/spiritual care:* Stay in touch with friends and their children.

  ◦ Choose like-minded friends.

  ◦ Read uplifting books together.

  ◦ Talk about them together, even with the little ones playing close by.

*Write your thoughts and Talk with your partners.*

- Invite another parent of a baby/toddler close to your child's age to come for tea, or plan to meet in the park. See if you can make this a regular visit. If you live close to a Waldorf School or other school with similar values, plan to join parent/child classes: a perfect way to meet like-minded parents, to learn a little about rhythmic home-life and for your child to begin learning the ins and outs of social life.

- On your family play day go for a picnic in the park with another family, or hike with small ones in back-packs.

- Parenting is hard work. Talk with your fellow parents about this journey. Share your joys and sorrows. Don't be drawn into parent conversations that devolve into competitions. Yes, this can begin in babyhood: who got a tooth first, who rolled over soonest. Our society would have us believe that hurrying begins at birth!

- Don't hesitate to get help, if you are feeling overwhelmed. We do not live in a parent and child-friendly world, so find a good therapist if you feel overcome with doubt or frustration.

• *Intellectual/Spiritual Self-bare:* Choosing like-minded friends will often fulfill at least part of your need for intellectual & spiritual stimulation; they will read the books you might be interested in or will have heard an intriguing podcast. Book discussion groups can be rewarding. Try this: invite three friends to read a book you love. Get together in each other's living rooms or in the backyard, each week and discuss one chapter. As the children play, you really *can* talk about subjects that interest you and still give small ones the attention they need. It will be good practice, to be able to hold a thought while caring for the little one, and then return to finish your sentence. The key is to keep the group small, and the number of children as well.

**Weekly Pages:** Which small increment did you begin with, in physically caring for yourself? How did this feel? An extra half-hour of sleep? A little protein for breakfast? Five minutes of yoga? Describe how you cared for yourself socially and what this nurturance feels like. Is your mind feeling a little brighter? How did you accomplish this?

**Conversation Notes:** Share with your partners you successes and your challenges. No self-recrimination allowed; face the difficulties with humor and acceptance. Laugh with each other, as you chart your course!

## Week Four Interactive Exploration

*This week we return to the place where we began. We deepen into the Heartfulness Meditation and the Heartfulness way of living with young children. We will experience this quiet loving heart as the foundation of discipline, for both our children and ourselves.*

- Choose a quiet time and place to practice the Hearfulness Meditation. Quietly breathe through the heart with the felt experience of goodness. Do this for five to ten minutes.
- Like before, on a large piece of crayoning paper, color with crayons the inner experience, the energy, the image of this meditative experience. Make images of your family's journey through this creation of Family Culture.
- Again sit back and gaze with open awareness at your image. Remember this image is an icon, it is a visual map that shows you where you have traveled, as you have been practicing the felt experience which heart coherence brings.
- Take a pen and blank piece of paper. Referring to the icon, write some new poetic words, they will act as an affirmation of your process. Again put these words on the refrigerator, or the bathroom mirror. Perhaps tape them on your computer, next to the first poem you wrote...give them a place to live in your daily life.
- Throughout the week, take a moment each day to look at the image and your poem; allow them to be the map that takes you to the place in which the breath moves through your heart.
- Feel gratefulness arise, as you become aware of the length this journey has taken you. Be aware of how your family has grown, since you first began. Smile...say ahhhh...

---

### Week Four Exploration

#### *We end where we began: Heartfulness*

- Practice Heartfulness for five minutes
- On drawing paper, make images of your inner experience and your family's journey.
- Gaze with open awareness.
- Write a new poetic rendering. Post these in your life.
- Each day look at your icon and your poem; they are your map.
- Feel gratefulness for the journey.
- Smile... say ahhh...
- Your heart is the foundation of your inner discipline and your compass through disciplinary moments.
- Congratulate yourself and enjoy!

*Write your thoughts and Talk with your partners.*

- Gaze at your image, read your poem and breathe. Let them visually transport you to the goodness heart breathing brings.
- Know this is the foundation of your own discipline as well as your approach to discipline with children.

**Weekly Pages:** You have come a very long way! Notice and describe how the Heartfulness Meditation, and practicing it with eyes open, has changed the way you live as a family. How have you subtly become more yourself, in this process? How has your family benefitted?

**Conversation Notes:** Talk with your partners about the way the meditation has changed as you have been practicing. And how you have changed in response to this practice. Celebrate this growth!

# WEEKLY PAGES

# CLOSURE
## STEP BACK AND ASSESS

Now is a good time for you to look at the huge amount of terrain you and your family have traversed since you began this trek. Here are some ways for you to take a little distance and appreciate the enormous consciousness and detailed work you have accomplished.

- Review, section-by-section, the topics you have worked with. Go back to your weekly pages and notice what areas of change have really "taken root." You will be amazed at how power-fully these small incremental changes make big impacts in the joy and fulfillment your family experiences together!

  - Just last week, you reviewed the *Heartfulness Meditation* and way of life, and you wrote this into your weekly pages. Continue this practice of writing your thoughts, as you continue to look back, to see how far you have come.
  - Think about and write how your inner rhythm and your *Family Rhythms* have changed. Notice the ripple effect; what has changed in response to this?
  - Consider how bringing joy into your daily and weekly *Family Work*, and how decluttering time and space have benefitted all.
  - Rejoice in your fine-tuning of *Family Play!* Notice how play-fulness lightens the load for everyone.
  - Congratulate yourself for being brave and joining your child in their *Artistic Experience*. Look through the files of your child's art-work; these will become family heirlooms.
  - Notice subtle ways your own creative mind has blossomed, now that you can tell your child homemade *Stories*.

---

Take a step back and look at the road your family has traveled together!

- Review section by section your topics.

- Reread your weekly pages. What has really "taken root"?

- Be amazed by your increased hearfulness on a daily basis.

- Notice how your inner rhythm and family rhythms are more balanced.

- Consider the joyfulness in your work and de-cluttering time and space.

- See the way playfulness lightens everyone's day

- Look through your child's artwork with him. Appreciate it together.

- Read some of your hand-made stories; write more!

- Marvel how your child's creative play has blossomed with her open-ended play space.

> *Bring all of this assessment to your partners. Celebrate!*
>
> *Write a summary, or a poem, or make a picture, or write a song to tell the tale in just the right way!*

- Marvel at your children's vast expanse of creative imagination, as they step into an entire childhood exploring the world of *Creative Play*. Pat yourself on the back for giving them the gift of open-ended play spaces.

- Now bring all this assessment to your partners. Share with each other, laugh and celebrate.

- Now write a Summary of all your experiences, emotions, thoughts about this process. Write this on the final Summary Pages. Or maybe write a poem, or make a picture, or write a song to tell the tale in just the right way!

# Summary Pages

# PAY IT FORWARD

Are you familiar with the expression "pay it forward"? Wikipedia tells us "'Pay it forward' is an expression for describing the beneficiary of a good deed repaying it to others instead of to the original benefactor. If you have enjoyed this process, share it with friends. Lend your workbook out; talk about what you have gained while you are on your work break; share your thoughts at family gatherings!

This simple, practical, soulful way of parenting is a very well-kept secret in the midst of the hectic clutter and rush of twenty-first-century life. Let your friends and family know who you are and what you value, without talking in abstract concepts. You can talk with them in very down-to-earth terms, for instance talk about the fun of sharing meals together while telling stories of your childhood to your children. Talk about the wonder of a regular bedtime and a well-slept child. Take photos of your children as they are busy at their amazing creative play, and show them around. You get the idea: Share the joy and *Pay It Forward!*

# Notes

1   Daniel Siegel, *The Whole Brain Child*, New York, Bantam Books, 2012, p. 24.

2   Newberg and Waldman, *How God Changes Your Brain*, New York, Ballantine, 2009.

3   From www.umassmed.edu/uploadedFiles/cfm2/Psychiatry Resarch_Mindfulness.pdf Accessed 10-1-2014.

4   This first section is an excerpt from my forthcoming book on the human brain.

5   From www.cdc.gov/niosh/docs/2004-143/pdfs/2004-143.pdf, "Work load Increase in US."

6   From www.en.wikipedia.org/wiki/Working_time, "Increase of Productivity 400 percent since 1950."

7   From www.economist.com/node/10329261, "Death by Overwork"

8   From www.cdc.gov/niosh/docs/2004-143/pdfs/2004-143.pdf, "Overwork and Health Repercussions."

9   See The New Games Foundation, *The New Games Book: Play Hard, Play Fair, Nobody Hurt*; and *More New Games!...and Playful Ideas.*

10  Bruno Bettelheim, *The Uses of Enchantment: The Meaning and Importance of Fairy Tales* (New York: Knopf, 1989), p. 7.

11  Carla Hannaford, *Smart Moves: Why Learning Is Not All in Your Head* (Arlington, VA: Great Ocean Publishers, 1995), p. 30.

12  Ibid., p. 95.

13  Carla Hannaford, op. cit., p. 27.

Also by Sharifa Oppenheimer

## *Heaven on Earth*
### A Handbook for Parents of Young Children

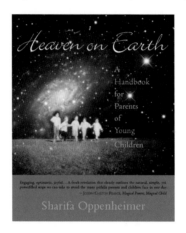

*Heaven on Earth* balances a theoretical understanding of child development with practical ideas, resources, and tips that can transform family life. Readers will learn how to create the regular life rhythms needed to establish a foundation for learning; how to design indoor play environments that allow children the broadest development of skills; and how to create outdoor play spaces that encourage vigorous movement and a wide sensory palette. Through art, storytelling, and the festival celebrations, this book is an invaluable guide to building a "family culture" based on the guiding principle of love—a culture that supports children and encourages the free development of each unique soul.

Photographs by Stephanie Gross
256 pages | 7½ x 9 | Paperback
SteinerBooks | $25.00
ISBN 978-0-88010-566-8